LEADING with Heart

Powerful Wisdoms
for lasting leadership in
Network Marketing

©2016 Todd Burrier

2/19/18

Diane —

Every now and then God winks at us through certain people He puts in our lives. You my friend, are a wink I am immeasurably grateful for.

Many Blessings,
Todd

THE BUSINESS OF NETWORK MARKETING HAS ALLOWED ME TO LIVE A LIFE I NEVER WOULD HAVE DREAMED POSSIBLE IN MY YOUTH.

Table of Contents

Introduction 3
Leadership is a Choice 7
It's all about Serving 9
Winning the Opportunity to Lead 11
Credibility is a Perception 13
The Engine of Credibility 15
Influence 17
Influence's Partner 18
The Microscope 19
Character 21
Know Thyself 23
Interpersonal Communication 27
Thinking Abundantly 31
Forgiveness 33
The Three Circles 35
Unplugging 38
Good-bye Excuses 40
Protecting the Trust 42
Time Utilization 45
Protecting Your Time 47
Time Allocation 49
Front Side Time 51
Communicating with the Network 53
Working ON versus Working IN 55

Financial Prudence 58
Specifically What Makes Them "Want to?" 60
Ask the Right Questions 62
Lead Them Where THEY Are............................65
Patient Frustration 68
Praise Power...73
Keep Your Old Shoes..75
Be a CEEO 77
It's Not About Motivating.................................81
Coaching in Leadership 85
"It's Not Working" 88
Comparative Caution 90
Dealing with Conflict 92
Protecting the Asset..96
Team Spirit...100
The Value of Vision 102
No Control..104
Leading in a Growth Phase 106
Leading Through Plateaus 110
Heart and the Crystal Ball...............................114
Final Thoughts 118
Addendum..122
End Notes 125
More Material 126

Introduction

I started my journey in network marketing two weeks before my son was born. Three months ago he turned 26. It blows my mind when I stop to look back. How could it have been so long ago? If you had told me when I came out of college that I would have a career in network marketing, I would have looked at you like you had two heads. Well, first I would have said "what's that?" And then after you told me, I would have looked at you like you had two heads!

The idea that I would be an entrepreneur? That I would be in a business where it was all about communicating and building relationships with people? Shy me? The guy with little self-esteem and zero discipline and a history of quitting everything? The guy who grew up putting electrical tape on his Chuck Taylors to cover the holes in them? What a preposterous idea that would have been for my brain to embrace.

If you would have gone further and said "not only will you have a career in the industry, but you will lead people and teach people. You will address crowds into the thousands at a time." Me? The guy who is so afraid to speak in front of people that he begged the Dean of his Economics Department in College to let him take extra English classes so he didn't have to take Public Speaking? The guy who is a true and proven lemming? The guy who is afraid to speak up to anyone and stand up for himself? I would no longer have been looking at your two heads, because at that point I would have been rolling on the ground laughing until I cried!

It's funny how life works out sometimes isn't it? So how did I get here? I'll give you the short version. After college, having little ambition at the time, I continued to work as a bartender because it was fun. After some years of that, it was time to get a "real job" (as my Mother called it) and I ended up in the real estate banking industry. About four years later, after getting laid off (by this time I was married with a child on the way), I was disillusioned and trying to figure out what to do next. I ended up in a network marketing opportunity meeting. It wasn't the first time I had been approached about network marketing, but it was the first time I was really open to learning about it. And my eyes were opened in a big way.

The business of network marketing has allowed me to live a life I never would have dreamed possible in my youth. Of course it hasn't always been easy, nothing of value is. But it has been an amazing blessing. Besides the cool lifestyle it has afforded, it helped me to discover many things about myself. One of the discoveries is my passion for teaching-and specifically, teaching leadership. And even more specifically, network marketing leadership.

You see, when you build a successful and lasting network marketing business, it's not just a way to make money, it's a vehicle that can provide the free time to explore anything in life that is on your heart to explore. For many people this is why they CHOOSE network marketing, because there are other things they want to do in life and they don't want to have to worry about earning an income daily when they pursue those things.

Anyway, for several years I was working in a leadership capacity in my network marketing business and making lots of mistakes. So I began studying leadership, applying what I learned to see what worked practically, and then teaching what I was learning. Then I furthered my education (MBA), began getting invited to teach leadership to companies of all sizes in Corporate America, and continued teaching leadership across the globe in network marketing. I absolutely LOVE to teach people about how to lead or be a better leader. I can do this all day and it feels like it's only been a few hours to me. Because the possibility that maybe someone in the crowd could take even one nugget of something I say, and it could help to change their life, the lives of their family, the lives of those they lead, and the lives of their families, and on and on, is so fulfilling that it's difficult to put into words. I have never figured out a better way to feel good than giving of myself to help serve someone else. The Old Testament proverb says it all "He who waters, will himself be watered."(Prov. 11:25)

So that leads me to this book. I know there are lots of books available about how to build a network marketing business. When I say network marketing in this work, I am talking about, referral marketing, network marketing, Multi-level Marketing, party plans, and direct selling. While they all may have nuances that separate them a bit, from the perspective of leadership they are the same. However, there are very few books about the ins and outs of leading an organization. Once the seed of writing this started to germinate in my heart, I had no choice but to do it. I attempted to create this in such a way that you can pick it up and look at different sections when you want to or when they are applicable. I struggled greatly on how much to include. This could be literally ten times the size it is, but I'm not trying to give you a leadership bible that is a huge, unwieldy, intimidating text book. I wanted you to have a practical, quickly applicable book that you could use immediately. So that's what I went for here. I hope it serves you and makes a difference.

So where does the process of becoming a leader start? It starts *in* you. You can not expect someone to follow you, if you are not certain *you* would follow you. Becoming a leader is a multi-faceted evolution. You have to do your part to *grow* as a leader, *demonstrate* that you are a leader, and then others have to choose to follow, and then you must *actually* lead.

The simple truth is this: you are only a leader if others are choosing to follow you.

In developing your leadership in network marketing you are cultivating the purest form of leadership. True leadership means there are "want-to" followers. You see, we all grow up in a world that is filled with structural hierarchy. We are constantly under the authority of those in a higher position and we have to do what they say. This occurs in our homes as a child, in school, at our job, in the government, the military, at church, and lots of other places. Most organizations of hierarchy are structural pyramids where each level down must do what is demanded by those above them. It's a normal, accepted, part of life. We are accustomed to being under someone's position of authority, and to the extent of that authority, and within its context; we have to do what we are told. This is whether we agree or not, whether we like it or not and whether we feel like it or not. Otherwise, there will be formal, predictable consequences. We don't feel as if we have a lot of choice.

Does this make those, whose rule we must follow, leaders? No.

It simply means they have a position of authority over us. They *might* be leaders, but that is not determined by the authority position. Whether or not they *are* leaders is determined by factors that inspire the person beneath them in the authority structure to want to follow. "Have to" versus "want to" is the primary distinction. In your network marketing business not a single person has to follow you. Everyone is their own boss. They will only follow you to the extent that they believe it will help them succeed in achieving their goals and they believe it's the best thing to do.

When you first sponsor someone, you are naturally looked to as a guide because most of the time you have been in the business at least a few days longer. It makes sense for the new person to want you to tell them what steps to take and where to find certain information. It's the closest thing to positional authority that exists. You are their sponsor, but you are not their leader. To be seen as a leader will take time and dedication. I'll walk you through the important aspects of the evolution through the pages that follow. My goal is to provide you with a concise and practical guide to building your ability to lead, such that as you develop your business, it is built on a foundation that will last a lifetime.

Leadership is a Choice

Is it possible to build a large organization without being a leader? I love asking this question to groups and then watching the different reactions. There are usually as many emphatic head shakes (no) as there are head nods (yes). So what is the answer? Yes, but. At its core, the business side of networking is directly tied to numbers. You *could* recruit so many people that eventually you'd find people who would grow a large business without any input from you. So YES, but...would you want to do this?

Those taking this no leadership approach may end up making a lot of money for a time, but it will be a lonely road. Network marketing is relationship centered. It's truly *relationship* marketing. Ultimately, since they are doing nothing for the organization, the organization will grow to resent them and feel used. Without the relationships there is no loyalty, and therefore no long term stability. The most important thing in any business is the people, not the products, marketing plan, or company attributes. At times of adversity in the field, people will leave to find another opportunity in droves if there is no relationship connection to leadership.

The other downside to choosing the no leadership road is that it's empty. Ask any true leader in the industry and they will tell you that the money is great, but there is nothing like the feeling you get when you know you have made a huge difference in someone's life by helping them. When you receive a paycheck for your work, it feels good. If it's a big check, it might feel really good! That feeling will not last very long though, and the money will soon be spent. Now consider the feeling you get when someone shares with you, with tears of joy in their eyes, the impact you have made on their life and the lives of those they care about! This feeling lasts for a long time. It fills you up. Each time you interact with this person you feel it. This is the true fruit. This is totally missed by the self-centered business builder (I didn't say self-centered leader because I believe that's an oxymoron!)

Ask any true leader in the industry and they will tell you that the money is great, but there is nothing like the feeling you get when you know you have made a huge difference in someone's life by helping them.

You *choose* to be a leader. It is not an easy choice, I admit, because it represents taking on enormous responsibility. But the fruit of the relationships and the lasting effects, on your business and life, are worth the choice. It is the same with anything else of value in life. The more of yourself you give, the more you receive, the more tears you cry, the more joy you have. If you want to build an organization for a lifetime, you must choose to become a leader.

The good news is that you *can* become a leader. Your DNA does not determine whether or not you can lead. You decide this personally. You will learn to lead in your own style, using your own set of gifts. You will learn to use your strengths as your foundation to thrive in leadership, and you will learn how to offset where you are weak. All leaders have both strengths and weaknesses.

Your decision to lead is the first step in *becoming* a leader. From there it's just a matter of putting in the time and effort. All leaders are born. But they are not born as leaders. They choose it.

Are you ready to make the choice to be a leader?

It's all about Serving

The opportunity to lead is actually the opportunity to serve. True leadership is about serving others. And this is especially the case in leadership of *volunteer* organizations, which is exactly what a network marketing organization is. I have heard it said that to lead at the highest levels, you have to be willing to serve at the lowest. This is an absolute truth when leading volunteers. For example, a true network marketing leader doesn't think about how many levels deep a person is, they only recognize that someone needs help and support and provides it. They know helping anyone helps everyone. I've seen so many instances in my career of someone being ignored by "leaders" because they were too deep. I've supported people all over the world in sidelines because they couldn't get their upline "leaders" to return their phone call. If I use quotations around the word leader it means NOT LEADER! How can you ignore someone who is asking for help? I don't know. I can't relate. Leaders serve if they can.

If you are not familiar with this philosophy, it's called *Servant Leadership*. Some of the most powerful leaders in history that left a lasting legacy were servant leaders. Think about Mother Teresa for example, and about how many people she positively impacted in her lifetime, and then many millions more after her lifetime, and into the future. I'm not inferring you should start living in the slums of Calcutta. I'm simply exampling how powerful a serving heart is.

Author and Leadership Guru, Ken Blanchard says "Servant leaders want to make a difference in the lives of their people and, in the process, impact the organization."* Which in turn, leads to a pretty good life for the leader!

"Servant leaders want to make a difference in the lives of their people and, in the process, impact the organization."

KEN BLANCHARD

Lots of people have the misconception that you work your way to the top and then, because you are the big leader, everyone will serve you. Not even close. This comes from the hierarchy conditioning I referred to earlier. Servant leadership flips the hierarchy upside down. The leader is at the bottom and the organization grows up and out on top of him or her. The bigger it gets the more the leader serves.

Remember everyone in the organization (downline) is choosing to be there, and choosing to follow you (if they do). Their primary interest is in getting where they are trying to go in the business. If they believe following you is the best way to do that, they will. But they have no interest in serving you. You must serve them. Think of it in this way. A shepherd is not served by his/her flock. The shepherd is tasked with the responsibility to take care of the sheep. It's the purpose of the shepherd. You, as the leader, are the shepherd. Many of the most influential leaders in the networking industry are servant leaders.

Consider some of the leaders you know in your life, which ones example a servant's heart?

Winning the Opportunity to Lead

You can choose to become a leader, but you can't make someone follow you. You have to be given the opportunity. It's like getting permission. Leadership expert Max De Pree, in his book *Leadership is an Art*, sums it up when he says "To be a leader means, especially, having the opportunity to make a meaningful difference in the lives of those who permit leaders to lead."* So how do you win this opportunity to lead? It would be great if you could just say "Hey, I'm the ticket! Follow me and all your dreams will come true!" and then they just follow. That's not going to happen. You have to *demonstrate* that you are a person that is worthy of being followed. The key word is *credibility*. You cannot proclaim that you are credible. You must show that you are. As speaker and author John Maxwell says, "Credibility is a victory not a gift."

> *"To be a leader means, especially, having the opportunity to make a meaningful difference in the lives of those who permit leaders to lead."*
>
> — MAX DE PREE

The great thing about credibility is that anyone can develop it, starting today. My friend Paul Welliver says "repetition, repetition, repetition, *reputation*." I don't know where Paul heard that, I only know I heard it first from him, and I never forgot it, because it is exactly how you develop credibility. You repeatedly do the right thing the right way while treating people well, people notice, and you begin to develop the reputation for whatever right thing you are doing. Simple!

In general, developing your credibility is a result of demonstrating competency in the area being assessed, and displaying good character. Think of it this way, competency is related to what you do and how you do it, and character is associated with who you are. You have to have both or you won't be credible. In network marketing you have to demonstrate competency in the areas that build a business. I call these the core competencies. These are the competencies of *The Process* which are used to build the business (making contacts, presenting information, etc.).

In order to be considered credible, you have to consistently demonstrate both competence and character. If you have one without the other, you will not be credible. For example, if I sponsor you and I am the nicest guy you ever met, but I'm clearly incompetent in the skills of building the business (you only signed up because you could see the opportunity despite me!), am I credible in the business? On the other hand, if I'm highly skilled, so much so that you are in awe of how smooth I am, but I am pressuring you and it is clear that I only care about myself; do I have credibility with you? The answer is obviously no in both areas. You need both to become credible.

The more credible you become in life in general, the more opportunities you will have. The more credibility you have in network marketing, the more opportunity to lead you will have.

Think about opportunities you have been offered in all aspects of your life. Were they a result of credibility you had already demonstrated in some way?

Credibility is a Perception

As you demonstrate the competence and character that provides you with the opportunity to lead, it's crucial that you understand that your credibility is purely a perception. You will be *perceived* as credible. I love Warren Buffet's words "When the tide goes out you see who is swimming naked" because they ring so true. Anyone can present an image that looks good on the surface, but what's really underneath? We learn not to judge a book by its cover, but I think often we still do this, especially when it comes to judging someone that presents themselves well. I have been fooled more than a few times by the "shiny leader" who was all charisma but little substance.

> *"When the tide goes out you see who is swimming naked."*
>
> — WARREN BUFFET

Those you lead will be basing everything they believe about you on their observations of, and interactions with, you. Anyone who is skilled at the work, and understands the technique of interacting with people can appear credible. Unfortunately, this doesn't show the heart or the deeper motivations. When things are going well, the credibility looks quite real. Smooth seas don't test the sailor too much. But at some point, as in all things in life, the seas get rocky and stormy. Now it becomes about who the sailor really is. You cannot fake it through difficulty. Who you are shows up clearly when the going gets rough. This tests the perception. When this happens you want to be at *least* as good as it is believed you are, if not better. Remember, life gives you the test and then gives you the lesson. By focusing now on the lessons, you will be a prepared and genuine leader such that when the test comes, it will simply be an opportunity to show what you've really got.

My wish for you is to develop into an awesome, inspiring leader that helps endless people reach their goals and improve their lives. The only way to ensure this is to devote yourself daily to becoming the best you can personally be. Challenges will reveal who you are already, not what you are working on becoming. This is why I am such a proponent of daily personal development. *The most challenging person you will ever lead is the one in the mirror.* In order to lead yourself well, you have to be purposeful in developing yourself. I began over 25 years ago to invest daily in my own development. I started with 15 minutes per day. It absolutely changed my life because it changed the way I thought and behaved. Over the years I went from just reading to help my mind to every aspect of developing and taking care of myself. Eventually it became much more time per day but it is the best investment I've ever made. You are worth the time to develop and grow yourself. Know this- regardless of what you have accomplished so far in your life, you are capable of so much more than you know. Wouldn't it be cool to find out? See the appendix for my Daily Dozen. The 12 things I personally do daily to grow and care for myself that have paved the way for me.

What hardships have you been through that you know made you better, and how did it make you better?

The Engine of Credibility

The engine of credibility, the thing that drives it to whatever level you obtain can be summed up in one word: trust. The greater the trust the network has in you, the greater your credibility. The greater your credibility, the more powerful your voice is. High credibility means your opinion matters to people. The authors of the book *Influencer* call this an opinion leader. Here's what they say about opinion leaders: "First these people are viewed as knowledgeable about the issue at hand. They tend to stay connected to their area of expertise, often through a variety of sources. Second, opinion leaders are viewed as trustworthy. They don't merely know a great deal about a certain area, but they also have other people's best interest in mind. This means that they aren't using their knowledge to manipulate or harm, but to help."* Opinion leaders are trusted in competency and character. They are credible because of the trust.

Credibility takes time to develop because trust takes time to develop. Trust grows slowly and it grows in layers. You learn to trust someone to a certain extent until they demonstrate that they can be trusted to a higher extent. Think about it this way. There are some people who you would not mind if they were in the street in front of your house but not in your yard. Then there are some who could be in your yard but not in your house. Then there are some who could be in your house, but only your foyer. Then there are others who could be anywhere in your house, as long as you are also in the house. Then there are some who could stay in your house while you are not there. I know this is elementary, but it is an example of how it is layered. Anyone could work their way from the street to the house, through earning trust.

Relative to establishing your credibility in the network, competency trust is simple in the beginning. The act of sponsoring your new business partner demonstrates competency to some degree. They can see it through the process of steps you took to sponsor them from the initial contact up until the time they became involved. This grows further as you begin to work with them and you provide insight as they work the process. They can see that you know what you are doing.

Character trust is much more difficult to achieve. It takes a substantial amount of interaction over time in a variety of circumstances to believe deeply in someone's character. I know a leader who has had people express to him over the years that at first it was hard to believe he was the kind of person he was presenting himself as being (nice, honest, and respectful). It's a little sad that people struggle with this, but it's true. The world around us is full of false pretenses, so experience has taught many people to be jaded, and with good reason because most everyone has been taken advantage of before. So literally, some people didn't trust him at first because they *couldn't believe* that he could be a good person! On the other side though, he has shared with me how good it feels when they come back at a later time and say that they realize that is just who he is. That doesn't make him unattainably special. Being nice and honest and respectful is easy to do and everyone can do it. The really good news is that demonstrating this consistently puts you in a different light than many people in the world. And it's a really good light to be in.

It takes a substantial amount of interaction over time in a variety of circumstances to believe deeply in someone's character.

Here's what you must know about the delicate nature of trust: if you break a competency trust, it can be rebuilt by simply improving yourself through practicing and working in the process, because others will clearly see the improvement and the results. Character trust on the other hand, is the area of trust that grows the slowest, and is the most easily damaged. Most of the time if you break a character trust, you break the relationship. It is just so personal that it is extremely difficult to repair and often you are not given a chance to repair it. People will leave you as a leader and many times they will leave the organization. This point is so important to being an effective leader that I will cover key trust and character issues later.

Think about the people in your life from each layer of trust I described. How long has it taken them to get to that layer, and what in their character has them in that layer?

Influence

When I am teaching leadership in workshop settings, I often ask the class to write down their definition of leadership. Then we go around the room and each person will share their definition. It's an interesting exercise that everyone likes, because of the differences in perspectives. All of the answers tend to be good answers. You could even say that they are all right answers. They just usually aren't THE right answer!

My study of John Maxwell's works many years ago introduced me to the idea that leadership can be boiled down to one word: influence. Influence is THE right answer. There is nothing else that so perfectly and succinctly describes leadership. Perhaps you are thinking …wait a minute Todd, you've been talking about credibility being the key! This is true. I have been talking about how your credibility demonstrates your worthiness to be followed. Your credibility creates the opportunity to lead. However, I know lots of credible people who do not lead. They *could* lead, but they don't. You see, Influence is the *purposeful* application of credibility.

You don't exert your credibility with others-it is merely the perception of who you are. Influence is when you utilize your credibility as a door opener to move people towards accomplishing a purpose. In bureaucratic organizations the position of authority is purposefully applied to make the organization succeed (of course, the best leaders in these organizations use influence also). In network marketing the leader *must* use influence. There is no other choice. Your leadership can only happen through this mechanism.

Influence is the purposeful application of credibility.

Dictionary.com defines influence as: The capacity or power of persons or things to be a compelling force on or produce effects on the actions, behaviors, opinions, etc. of others.

When a person of high credibility makes a suggestion or offers advice or rallies people for a cause, the people with interest in the subject are likely to be compelled to act. This is influence in action. The most successful leaders in history in all areas of life were leaders through influence.

With whom are you purposefully applying your credibility right now?

Influence's Partner

In the position of a servant leader, the greater the size of the organization, the greater the responsibility of the servant leader. Having influence requires being responsible to ensure it is asserted in a positive way. This is part of where the proof of credibility comes into play. There are many examples of leaders in the world, especially in political arenas, who obtained a strong position of leadership then used this position purely as a platform to serve themselves at the expense of those they should be serving.

Influence is the greatest of power. Like the pied piper of the fabled tale. It can be used for good or evil. You play your pipe of influence and people follow. The greater the influence the more quickly they follow. Influence should always be balanced with responsibility. A leader considers the overall impact of anything they bring to the organization.

Influence should always be balanced with responsibility.

I talk about this point because I want you to have clarity that your decision to become a leader is a decision to accept all the responsibility that goes with the territory. Your influence will impact many people's lives significantly. Those you serve will make decisions that will affect the future of their families based upon their belief in you. They will champion the business in such a way that it will touch many others. This is a great responsibility.

Have you ever made a decision that impacted several people (because of your influence) only to find out that you had not considered the consequence that occurred?

The Microscope

As a leader, you are under a microscope. Your organization is constantly watching you closely. The more you *do what you say*, the more your influence will grow and the better leader you will be. One of the greatest compliments you can receive from someone in your organization is for them to tell you that you truly walk your talk.

It's vital to understand that this microscope is not just relative to your work. It is about you as a complete person. You will be gauged in all areas of your life and in all types of situations. Business coach and author Dave Martin says "As a leader, you must be a good role model. You must always conduct your life as if everybody is watching you. You must keep your word always. You must be consistent in the way you treat people, never regarding one person as more important than another and always respecting those around you, regardless of their status in life."* I'll never forget a phone conversation I had with a man in Florida several years ago that illustrates this point. Many years prior to this conversation (at least 10 years) I was speaking at a large weekend event in Atlantic City, New Jersey and he was attending the event. He did not really know me yet, but he was in the organization and knew of me. He shared with me that what made the biggest impact on him at the event was not anything I said from the stage, it was something he saw me do. I was curious because I had no clue what he was talking about so I asked him to elaborate. He told me that during a break he was headed around a corner and he saw me in the lobby helping someone with a disability to get on an elevator. There was no one else in the lobby, according to him, so he knew I wasn't helping this man to impress anyone. I never knew he was watching. Truth be told, I had no recollection of doing what he said I did! He shared with me, that at that moment, he knew I was a person he could believe in.

One of the greatest compliments you can receive from someone in your organization is for them to tell you that you truly walk your talk.

The microscope applies in your community as well. Everywhere you go and everything you do, someone is watching. You may be at the grocery store interacting with the clerk, or strolling down the aisle shopping. You must know that while someone in your organization might not be at the grocery store, someone from the community that is in the process or will be in the process of learning about your business could be. Many people will know who you are. They will have heard what a good person you are. Remember, your network is also talking about you with their contacts. Their contacts will also be watching you and not in the same way your organization is. They will be doubtful because they don't truly know yet how good our business is, and they don't really know you. Your behavior in the community will influence your long term business in a big way.

Behaving in a nice, honest, and respectful way at all times will further your entire organizations ability to grow your network community in the general community. It will help the community see what a great group of people your organization is. And it will increase your attractiveness. All this just because you went grocery shopping!

Have you ever seen someone treat another poorly in public? How did it make you feel?

Character

I heard this or read it somewhere: "Fall in love with looks and personality but marry character!" When you think about the leaders you follow, it's a little like marrying some of your future to what you believe about them in relation to where you are trying to go. What is it about them that makes you want to follow them? What is it you admire and respect? Now take that mindset and consider what *the best characteristics for leadership are?* This is both an easy question and a difficult one to answer. Everyone has a unique set of characteristics that come naturally, and has the ability to develop others. I've never met anyone who has every single desirable character trait there is. I've had leadership workshop groups identify as many as 80 different desirable characteristics in a single workshop!

The point is this: There is no blueprint for the perfect set of leadership characteristics. But there are some characteristics which I believe are essential for leading a network marketing organization. These are characteristics that readily affect how your character is perceived, so in essence they are the character traits that develop trust in the deepest way. Here are some of the most important:

Kindness: Servant leaders need to be approachable. Being nice makes people feel comfortable to be around you. You cannot lead people in a volunteer setting if they fear you, so you must be kind. Love your people and they will love you.

Honesty: This is the number one most desirable character trait of a leader. It is the most frequently mentioned in the workshops that I lead and of those leadership teachers I have studied. The word integrity could be used here as well.

The first two aren't negotiable. If you don't have these, get them or forget about ever being a long term leader. There are so many others that matter that it's pointless to try and list them all so I'll just give you some of the ones I value the most: respectful, authentic, humble, reliable, attentive, open-minded, self-disciplined, considerate, consistent, confident, helpful, understanding, committed, fair, loyal, courageous, visionary, and passionate. I'm sure you can think of a lot more and I probably left out a few you think are as important, or more important, than anything I listed. Whichever you think matters most, work on them, strengthen them, and let them help you grow your influence ability.

What are the characteristics you believe are the most important?

Know Thyself

I am imperfect and you are imperfect. I'm certain we can agree on this. So what is the value of knowing this? The obvious thing is we should be humble because we are all no better than each other and succeeding as a leader doesn't make us better than anyone. What it does do though, is put us more in a spotlight where our weaknesses are more readily visible.

It's important for all people to understand their strengths and weaknesses, and even more so for someone in a leadership position. If you have not assessed your personal strengths, you should do this immediately because this will reveal to you the things that will best serve you in succeeding. The more you operate in your strength areas the more effective you will be.

Your strengths will be found in your talents, gifts, skills, passions, knowledge, resources, and personality traits. By uncovering them you will have a deeper understanding of what you can use to grow. The Proverb says "A man's gifts makes room for him and brings him before great men."(Prov. 18:16) Your strengths *are* gifts and working with them will take you as far as you would like to go. Take some time alone and make a list of them all and then consider how to best use them in your business, as well as create a plan for further developing them. Working to develop areas in which you are strong is a multiplier for productivity because it *feels* so good to work in your strengths. Marcus Buckingham, in his book *Go Put Your Strengths to Work*, gives valuable insight when he talks about working hard for a long period of time using your strengths. He says, "You may feel physically tired, to the point where you are not yet ready to saddle up and tackle them all over again, but you don't feel psychologically drained. Instead you feel fulfilled, powerful, restored, the exact opposite of drained. It's a satisfying feeling sure, but it's also much more than mere satisfaction. It feels authentic, correct."* I know exactly what he is talking about. When I spend a full day teaching about building and leading a network, I may be physically fatigued, but I am psychologically lit up like a Christmas tree!

Your weaknesses present a different challenge. There is a tendency to believe that it's important to work on your weaknesses. For the most part, this is a false belief. Many areas of weakness exist because we aren't interested in these things or they are counter to our personality and behavior traits. Therefore, we've avoided them and they remain weaknesses.

As a general rule, especially in building a business, we should only work on the weaknesses that hinder our ability to use our strengths because these are the ones that are hurting our productivity. From a leadership standpoint, I often see leaders trying to hide their weaknesses. They try to appear as if they are closer to perfect than they are. This is a big mistake for two reasons. The first is that if you do a good job at hiding them, then you will seem too good for anyone to believe they could model you. The organization will see you as unattainable, because they are facing their own weaknesses on a daily basis. This is disempowering to them and provides an excuse to NOT build a business. After all, if they have to be as perfect as you to succeed there is no hope for them in their eyes. The second and bigger reason is that you probably won't be as good at hiding your weaknesses as you would like to be. Remember, you are under a microscope. Your weaknesses will be visible to those in the organization. Having weaknesses is a human, normal thing. Pretending you don't have weaknesses is inauthentic and lacks integrity. This violates trust.

As a general rule, especially in building a business, we should only work on the weaknesses that hinder our ability to use our strengths, because these are the ones that are hurting our productivity.

So what do you do? There are two specific things to do that are crucial. The first is to identify your weaknesses, and then have a strategy for addressing the ones that impact your effectiveness. Here are five strategies you can employ to overcome a weakness:

1) **Delegate:** In the organization you will have people who have strengths you don't have. This is an excellent opportunity to involve them. This shows them you have confidence and trust in them and builds them up as people. This will translate into helping them believe in themselves which will boost their action and their results.

2) **Ask for Help:** This shows you are real. You need help just like other people need help. The cool thing about this is that most people like the opportunity to help! In addition, many of the people in the organization would love to do something for you because of all you have done for them. This is a chance to let them give back and it will make them feel good.

3) **Out-source:** Your time is valuable. There are plenty of people that have skills in the areas you are weak that you could pay to do what needs to be done. If you broke this down to the true cost of your time in relation to the many hours it would take you to do the thing that is not in your strength area, you are actually making money by paying someone to do it, because your time is money!

4) **Use systems:** Many areas of weakness can be solved by inputting a system to manage it. This way the system does the work for you. It will take a little time in the front but save you countless hours of lost productivity and frustration going forward.

5) **Learn:** There will be some things that you will have to invest time in to learn to do adequately because *only you* can do these things. This is particularly true of weak areas in personality and behavior traits. This is what personal development is all about.

I have many weaknesses that if unaddressed would make building a business very difficult for me. I won't share them all with you, but I will give you a few examples. I mentioned earlier that I'm a natural introvert. This shows up in being shy and a bit socially awkward. As a result, listening is a natural tendency that I have personally developed into a major strength. However, in order to work the process and build a business it is necessary to make contacts. This is where the weakness shows up. Since this is the most important step to take as it initiates the entire process, I had to learn how to navigate social situations to be effective, as well as how to make direct contacts by phone. I worked long and hard at this because it was essential to succeed. I would never have been able to use the strength of listening if I could not engage people. This is why I teach such an authentic and comfortable approach, because I had to develop this out of necessity. The benefit of this is huge, because not only did it allow me to master this key fundamental, it provided a way for anyone, regardless of personality traits, to find a comfort zone in initiating contacts and working the process. I'm also not detail oriented, forgetful, and have poor organizational skills when it comes to things. This is a glaring weakness for working in the process because follow up is where most of the business occurs. I use systems to completely negate this weakness to the point where it appears to others to be a strength.

Take some time and address all the weaknesses that stand in the way of further success by identifying them and then applying the appropriate strategy to overcome them. You'll be glad you did this for yourself, as you will become even more effective than you already are, but you will also now have a template in which to help the people you serve work through their weaknesses.

The second thing to do is counterintuitive, and that is to openly share your weaknesses with the people in the organization. This will inspire them. They will see some of the real, relatable things you have had to work through to succeed. This will show them that they can work through theirs also and it will build deeper trust with them because you openly authentically share your imperfections.

What are your strengths and how can you use them more often in growing and leading your business?

Interpersonal Communication

Interpersonal communication skills are essential to being an effective leader. This is something you will need to study and practice on a consistent basis to develop into a strong leader. Study it? I already know how to communicate! I wouldn't blame you for thinking this way. You do know how to communicate or you likely wouldn't have gotten far enough in building a network to be reading this book! But do you really know how to communicate the most effective way possible such that you can interact in a highly effective and engaged way with anyone that crosses your path in all kinds of situations? Maybe, but probably not. How can I say this? Because interpersonal communication skills, the most important skills you could possibly have in a world where everywhere you look there are people, are not taught in educational curriculums. I hold a Master's degree in Business Administration. This is an advanced level of education. But at no point in my entire path of education was I required to take courses on interpersonal communication skills. The very skills that would help me to use the education in business I was receiving were not in the course work. We should be required to study and train in these skills from the time we start school at five or six years old until we finish whatever level of education we pursue. They are *at least* as important as any other subject we study.

These skills have to be at the top of your personal development list. Your personality is on display when you communicate whether you know it or not. We all have aspects of our personality that are positive *and* negative. Without the right training and development we struggle to reduce the impact of the characteristics we don't like and we're unable to utilize our strong points in an enhanced way. Your personality is either a blessing or a curse, depending on your level of personal development.

Your personality is either a blessing or a curse, depending on your level of personal development.

If you look across the business landscape in all industries you will find that the most technically skilled workers frequently work for someone who is not nearly as skilled but has excellent communication or people skills. Leadership is about achieving significant levels of success through the efforts of others. It has little to do with your own technical abilities. You can be average in your ability to work the process and still build a successful business, because it is simply a function of numbers. Leadership at the highest levels, however, demands that you master interpersonal communication because these are competencies that reflect as *character* issues.

An example of what I mean is the skill of listening. Hearing is a gift, but listening is a skill. Effective leaders are excellent listeners. But listening is challenging. By nature human beings are self-focused. In any conversation, once someone begins to speak we immediately are thinking about what we have to say. If we interrupt the other person we are essentially telling them (through our actions) that what we have to say is more important that what *they* have to say. We have devalued them. In leadership, this is a major relationship breaker. The people in your organization aren't thinking about whether or not you are a skilled listener. They are only considering how they feel when they speak to you. If you do not listen well, *they will see this in a variety of ways that all reflect the way they perceive your character*, regardless of how good of a human being you are. Since you are constantly under a microscope, you have to really develop this skill so that you are perceived in a high character, caring way. The last thing you want is to be considered self-important, or not caring, or stubborn, or inconsiderate. Listening is the king of the interpersonal skills because it can elicit all these perceptions and many more both positive and negative. My friend Gabi Winkler is the single best listener I have ever met. I love to watch Gabi listening to someone. She listens to them in such a way that they feel like the most important person in the world at that moment. Sometimes you can change a life just by listening. In the book The Road Less Traveled M. Scott Peck, M.D. shares the awesome power of listening when he says "In approximately a quarter of our cases, whether patients are adults or children, considerable and even dramatic improvement is shown during the first few months of psychotherapy, before any roots of problems have been uncovered or significant interpretations have been made. There are several reasons for this phenomenon, but chief among them, I believe, is the patient's sense that he or she is being truly listened to, often for the first time in years, and perhaps for the first time ever."* This is real world stuff. When you listen to someone its possible you are the first person to really do that for them in a long time. His book was written way before cell phones and texting, and instant messaging, which has created even more distractions during human interaction. I believe that people in general are emotionally starving from no one listening. Imagine how powerful it is to be someone who listens well in today's world, and then you can begin to see how this single skill can catapult you up the leadership ladder.

If you do not listen well, they will see this in a variety of ways that all reflect the way they perceive your character.

There are multiple facets to good interpersonal communication skills. In addition to listening, asking questions, body language, interpreting feelings, personality styles and tendencies, language and words, and more, are all part of interpersonal communication. Since societally there is no required formal training in these areas, we are products of our environment and experiences. This is too limiting and causes us to rely on only a few tools as opposed to having an entire communication tool box at the ready for any interaction.

We all encounter what I call the *communication gap* many times per day. The communication gap is the difference between what someone says and what the other person *thinks* they said. Without the right skills we have days full of miscommunication due to this gap. In leadership, the gap leads to people you communicate with in the organization feeling misunderstood or disconnected with you. As I said before, they will not assess this from a skills competence standpoint. They will see it from a character lens and it will inhibit your ability to lead them. Take some time each day and study and practice in this area and you will see your ability to lead any kind of person grow quickly.

What will you do today to become a better communicator?

Thinking Abundantly

I believe we are conditioned culturally to have a scarcity mentality. Participating in competition in school, economic markets, and sports, tend to drive this point more deeply into us. Often, someone has to win and someone has to lose. This is common in the workplaces of the people you will sponsor. Climbing over someone else to get ahead so you can *get yours before another can get theirs*. This fosters environments that are not cooperative and collaborative. We must rise above this as leaders. It is an abundant world. There is plenty of business for everyone to prosper. Someone *doesn't* have to lose for us to win. We can all win. We can all succeed at high levels and an abundance mentality is the optimal way to do this. The very essence of our work is to help others succeed as a stepping stone for our own success.

Someone doesn't have to lose for us to win. We can all win.

Scarcity mentality is fear based. It is a perspective that someone else accomplishing something in some way diminishes us and reduces the potential of our opportunities. I once heard it said that "there is plenty of gravy for all of us to drag our biscuits through." I love this analogy because it is so true. When we work with a spirit of abundance we work without fear of loss due to other's victories. We are able to celebrate and be joyful of other's achievements.

Jealousy and insecurity are two things that will weaken your ability to lead. These are also classic symptoms of a scarcity mindset. If these are issues for you then this is an area of personal growth that is important to address. You cannot show any kind of insecurity in leadership. As a leader, you are like a lighthouse. You stand strong and shine your light to provide guidance and reassurance on the journey to success. Lighthouses share their light with *all* ships. They don't consider what ship is better than another. They exist for all ships. Opportunity to flourish is as vast as the ocean. There are billions of people in the world, many of which will become a part of your organization provided it is a place that feels good.

This perspective applies to the industry as well as to the company you promote. You never have to tear anything, or anyone else, down to make yourself or your business look better. Focus on being the best *you* can be. Champion your company as what you believe is best for you. Let this be what you stand firm on. This will raise you above the muck where people are fighting and clawing at each other for scraps. Abundance is not about scraps. It is bountiful.

You never have to tear anything, or anyone else, down to make yourself or your business look better.

Consider how you feel when someone you know has a significant achievement. Are you genuinely happy for them?

Forgiveness

In leadership, people are going to hurt you. Speaker and author Joyce Meyer says "as leaders, we are never going to get anywhere unless we are ready to forgive people. It is something that we are going to have to do frequently."* Some people will do it purposefully and others will do it unintentionally. Initially the intention won't matter, it will hurt just the same. English poet, Alexander Pope said "To err is human, to forgive is divine." As a leader, developing a forgiving spirit will serve you well.

> *"As leaders, we are never going to get anywhere unless we are ready to forgive people. It is something that we are going to have to do frequently."*
>
> JOYCE MEYER

The person that hurts you without intention is easy to forgive. You can chalk it up to an innocent mistake, an error in judgement, or a lack of competence. These kinds of hurts happen the most and are not too difficult to forgive and recover from. But what about the person who intentionally hurts you?

This is where the real challenge exists. Our natural instinct might be to retaliate in some way or to hold a grudge and harbor resentment towards them. There have been a few times in my career when someone has purposefully done something with the intention of harming me in some way. I am a sensitive person so I feel these things deeply. You probably would too. It's also difficult for me to shake those feelings. I am not a retaliation kind of person, but I definitely tend to harbor feelings.

Eventually I learned that there is *no value* in harboring these feelings. Joyce Meyers says it well again when she says "I believe that when we refuse to forgive other people, we are the ones who end up in a prison of emotional torment." She speaks such truth in these words. For many years I let those feelings affect me. All because I couldn't forgive. At times it would affect my work. In essence, I allowed myself to be a prisoner to those feelings. In the biblical parable of the sower, the farmer knows that some of the seeds will be eaten by the birds. But the farmer doesn't chase the birds. He lets the birds have the seed and continues to sow more seed. Being unforgiving is like emotionally chasing the birds. It takes our minds away from sowing in the field. In leadership, *the field is the people we serve*. Any time we spend on negative non-productive things takes us away from serving others. We are not only hurting ourselves by doing this, we are hurting the people we are serving because our attitude is affected and so is our availability. By forgiving we are freeing ourselves to be our best.

If someone hurts you, move on. Forgive them. Let go of it. I'm not saying to forget it completely. An important part of growing your leadership ability is the wisdom you develop along the way. You now know a little more about this person, and to what level you can trust them, so from a practical standpoint you are careful in interaction and involvement with them. From a heart standpoint, you must forgive them and not dwell on it. There is no point throwing good energy after bad. Have a forgiving spirit and the hurt will flow away from you more quickly.

Who do you need to forgive?

The Three Circles

Self-discipline is a requirement for success in any aspect of life. Leadership requires self-discipline at the highest level. Any area of priority where you are undisciplined will undermine your ability to lead. It's not my place to tell you what your priorities should be. That is for you to decide. It is important however, to know which priorities will impact your ability to build your business and to lead others in doing so as well, and this is what the three circles are all about.

The three circles represent your business, your health, and your relationships. These three things need to be among your priorities because if they are not you will ultimately sabotage your own success. From a practical point of view the connection between the three is easy to see once you consider it. I remember vividly that early in my career I was so focused on building my business that my health and my marriage were suffering. Fortunately for me, I corrected my path before it was too late. But I have known many people who never corrected the path. They were so caught up in the business circle, that they payed too heavy of a price in the health and/or relationship circles. It is a sad unnecessary reality in all industries, but can easily be corrected in building a network marketing lifestyle because of the time freedom.

Your health will have a major impact on your ability to build your business successfully. Physical neglect leads to low energy and ultimately to health problems. It is not possible to perform at a high level when you are fatigued. Good nutrition, exercise, and rest are necessary to be able to perform at your best. These are disciplines that all long term leaders will have to develop. Fatigue leads to low emotional energy as well as low physical energy. As a leader, your energy is contagious in the network. Extended lack of discipline in personal health will lead to significant health problems. This would have a major impact on your ability to work in the business. Depending on the severity of the problem, it might eliminate your ability to work at all.

Your important relationships are also affected by the state of your health. Relationships require time and focused attention. It's difficult to focus on others when you don't feel well. If you are not taking care of your health you will use what energy you have to build your business and your relationships will suffer. Even if you do take care of your health, you have to be purposeful in prioritizing your important relationships. Neglecting your relationships will cause them to break down. When an important relationship breaks down it becomes emotionally paralyzing. Your ability to work will be dramatically impaired. You will have difficulty focusing because the trouble in the relationship will be constantly on your mind. Balancing this aspect of your life is further compounded because building a network is all about relationships. You will be dedicating time and attention to many people every day. This will be rewarding for you. It will fill you up emotionally at times and wear you out at others. Your daily need to be fed emotionally from your family relationships may not be as great because much of your relational needs are being met. This is not happening for your spouse or significant other unless they are working along side of you in the business. You have to be purposeful to take care of your family relationships first. This will strengthen your emotional platform and make you better at serving your organization. If your life partner is working with you it is still vital to have time where you turn the business off and just be a couple who love each other. This is part of what I call *unplugging*.

To further illustrate this point think of it this way. Does it make any sense to sacrifice something to succeed that is so precious that at the moment you lost it, you would gladly trade all of your success to get it back? This is the truth about health and relationships. Nothing on earth is more important than these two things. If you lost your health you would give away all your money to get it back. Same is true if you were to lose the love of your life. But if you lost all your money, you could simply start over and build again. Your level of success in life comes largely through who you become as a person. The more developed you become, the more easily you can replicate any level of success should you need to. You might not want to ever test this theory, but it's true. Take care of your health and relationships and you will flourish in life.

Does it make any sense to sacrifice something to succeed that is so precious that at the moment you lost it, you would gladly trade all of your success to get it back?

The three circles have a deeper impact on your leadership ability then their effects on your personal life. Earlier I talked about the microscope. This is a highly visible aspect of you as an example, because these areas will be on full display at all times. Self-discipline is represented in all three circles. The discipline required to build your business is self-evident. Without it, you are not even in the leadership position in the first place. The other two areas are essential as well. Think of it this way; you know that discipline is important. In front of you is a very competent person who is creating a successful business, but is neglecting their health or having trouble in their relationship. Doesn't it make you wonder if they are really what they are saying they are? *The whole person is always in front of you.* As a leader who is representing a possibility of a great lifestyle you must model it *completely*. Any breakdown in the three circles will cause others to question your authenticity. They will see you as presenting yourself one way in one area but not the same person in another. In essence, you would be damaging your credibility. This is poison to your ability to lead. Live every day in the three circles and you will impact the most people in the best way and be an attractive example as to what is possible to the organization.

Are you purposefully investing time regularly in the three circles?

Unplugging

Rest is necessary for any of us to function at our best. I'm not just talking about sleep. I'm talking about relaxing and letting your mind take a break. This is especially important for leaders. Leaders invest a lot of time pouring energy into others. It goes with the territory. This is one of the reasons the daily dozen (addendum) is so important. It is a way to pour back into yourself, because if you don't do it, there is no guarantee that anyone else will.

There are many thankless moments in leadership. Often, the people you serve will take for granted all that you do for them. This is why it is especially rewarding when others encourage you and let you know how working with you has made a positive difference in their lives- this pours energy back into you. There is also a tendency for leaders to work long stretches of time, several months in a row, or even a few years in a row, without really unplugging themselves from the network. This is a mistake seasoned leaders know intimately because they have all made it at some point. It is the nature of a leader to be a doer and to work long hours. It's how they have escaped the rat race, so to speak. The problem occurs when they turn their networking business into another version of the rat race! You have to unplug at times. It's vital for being the best long term leader you can be and it sets the best example for the organization. Successful leaders who have achieved all the material aspects of success (homes, cars, live in exotic locations, etc.) but appear to be constantly working, aren't inspiring others to emulate them. They have to demonstrate a balance of all the desirable lifestyle aspects they have earned. In today's world we are so connected that we can be working all the time from anywhere. This is a good thing because it makes a unique lifestyle more obtainable than ever, and it allows people more than ever to build the business in whatever hours they'd like.

You have to unplug at times. It's vital for being the best long term leader you can be and it sets the best example for the organization.

The downside of this occurs when we don't *stop* working! If we have meals with our family and we have our cell phone at the table, this is not good. If we take a phone call (or even check who's calling) during dinner with our family or read and respond to a text, we are sending a signal to the family that business is more important than they are. In time, this will create resentment of the business among the family. If we go to bed with our cell phones and our computers (for business purposes), this is not good. We are not allowing our minds to take a break and we will eventually burn out and become emotionally drained. So my advice is *do not take your business* to bed with you. Do not have your phone or get up to answer your phone when having meals with your family. It can wait. You need the break and your family deserves to have YOU with them.

In the bigger picture, take some scheduled time away. The world's not going to end because you don't work for a few days or even a few weeks. When you are in a building phase it's tempting to work every day of every week for months on end because *you can* and it's fun! Don't do this. Put some boundaries around your time. As a general rule, designate some times of the week where you are not available and let your organization know this. Every month or two schedule a long weekend to just play. This will be hard to do in the early stages of building your business because you might feel guilty about it. Get over it. It's too important for you and the people you care about.

Take at least a few long vacations per year where you are not available. This is needed for you to recharge yourself and it's important for the network to see this aspect of the lifestyle that they want to emulate. You work hard and pour into others constantly and you want to be able to do this for years to come. So take some time to unplug and refresh on a consistent basis. It's the best thing for you.

How will you unplug regularly to keep yourself fresh?

Good-bye Excuses

People who lead don't make excuses and people who make excuses don't lead. Excuses are credibility killers. Excuses aren't real. They are simply reasons we give for not doing the thing we should have done in the given situation. When I got this in my brain many years ago, it was a game changer for me. For much of my early life *I was a quitter*. I can look back now and point to my low self-esteem as a causal factor, but that doesn't change the fact that I was the quitter. I had an excuse for everything. Each time I quit or failed to achieve what I was capable of I would justify how it was someone else's fault that I couldn't go forward. Guess what those excuses got me? Absolutely nothing.

Once you accept the responsibility to lead you sacrifice your right to make an excuse. Excuses are part of the world around us. Think about all the excuses you hear from people you sponsor. They will give you all kinds of reasons to justify not taking action. They will tell you that they didn't have time, or that they don't know enough people, or they don't know how to do it, or they are too young, or too old, or not smart enough, or don't have any money, or they're too busy, or they don't know how to talk to people, or _____ fill in the blank. Excuse, excuse, excuse. None of these are real. These are choices.

Excuses are credibility killers.

Leaders choose to do whatever it takes. Every leader I know has fought and scratched through all kinds of difficult situations. They have overcome various internal struggles. They have done what they had to do. They could have made an excuse and it would have been accepted by the people around them because they make excuses too. They could have justified any level of inaction and it would have been okay with their friends and families. But it would not have been okay with them. They realized that if they were talking to themselves 20 years in the future and explaining why they accomplished little in comparison to what they could have accomplished in their life given their multitude of blessings and gifts, those excuses would be *hollow*. They would have no substance. They would be worthless.

Leaders know that the business of network marketing is blameless. There are no excuses worthy of not living the life you can live. Say good bye to your excuses forever and say hello to an amazing and exciting journey that leads to an awesome life!

Think about excuses you find yourself using. How will you eliminate them?

Protecting the Trust

I once heard it said, "You cannot talk your way out of something you behaved your way into." This statement speaks to the heart of protecting the precious trust you have developed with the people you serve. Jim Burke, former Chairman and CEO of Johnson and Johnson said, "You can't have success without trust. The word trust embodies almost everything you strive for that will help you succeed. You tell me any human relationship that works without trust, whether it is a marriage or a friendship or a social interaction; in the long run, the same thing is true about business, especially businesses that deal with the public."* In network marketing your business doesn't just deal with the public, it *is* the public! Yet, even if you are a person of the highest integrity, there will always be people who misinterpret your actions. It's simply the nature of interacting with lots of people who come from all types of backgrounds and environments. Since trust is at the foundation of your ability to lead, it is vital that you are as careful as possible to protect it. You cannot control what others think but you can control what *you* do and say. It is very easy to break the trust with someone and not even know that you have done so. There are many ways that this can happen; too many to write about here, as it would be an entire book all by itself. However, I would like to point out a few of them.

Mistakes: Everyone makes mistakes. It's not a question of whether you will make some but how you handle them. Leaders tend to make more mistakes during the course of business simply because they take initiative and make lots of decisions. Admit your mistakes and apologize if you have hurt someone.

Listening: One of the fastest ways to break trust in a relationship is to be perceived as not listening. If people think you don't listen they will feel that you don't respect them. They will feel de-valued. This is death to a relationship and to a leadership position.

Credit: Go to great lengths to give credit for anything and everything that others contribute. If someone in the organization brings you an idea that you implement, champion them as the one who brought it to you. If someone has some success, give them ALL the credit. Make sure the world knows that they did it, not you. This one is a challenge because as a leader you will be recognized for your achievements. Often your recognition is the result of others working hard and ascending to new levels of success. Make sure everyone knows you are being recognized because of the efforts and achievements of others.

Pressure: If it is perceived that you are pressuring people, you will be seen as self-serving-*even if your intentions are good.* Regardless of how much you want someone to succeed for *their* benefit they will believe you are pressuring them for *your* benefit. It's just the nature of the work. The minute you are seen as someone who is only interested in what you can get, as opposed to what you can give, you will have completely broken the trust.

Truth: Lying is never a good thing. You don't need me to point this out. Half-truths are equally dangerous, because they are deceitful, even if they appear harmless. 'Sugar-coating' falls into this category. Sometimes you will be tempted to only point out the good in a situation. This will not serve you or the person you are interacting with. It's better to put the entire issue on the table so it can be talked about transparently. Nothing is perfect. All businesses have challenges so don't pretend they are non-existent or you will look naïve or deceptive. Both of these will affect trust.

Keeping Confidences: As a leader you are working with many people and you will be trusted with information of all kinds. You will learn deep things about the people you work with. Sometimes you will learn things you would rather not know. You need to be a vault. If something is shared with you that's personal, it needs to be locked away and never spoken about to anyone else, including those closest to you.

Criticism: Never be critical of someone in front of others, either in their presence or when they are not with you. If you don't have something nice to say about someone, say nothing. If someone tries to pull you into a conversation about someone that is anything other than positive, let them know that is not something you are interested in discussing. The first time someone hears you speak poorly about others, they will assume you speak poorly to others about them.

The trust you build with your network is sacred and needs to be treated like gold.

This is just the tip of the iceberg on this topic. The trust you build with your network is sacred and needs to be treated like gold. Be conscious of your tendencies and know your weaknesses. I had to learn this the hard way over the years. I am someone who naturally likes people to feel good. This meant that I had a tendency to shy away from anything that might hurt their feelings, or disappoint them. I had to learn to just tell the truth whether they like it or not because in the long run this is best for all. I am a non-confrontational person. I had to learn to confront things that needed to be confronted rather than ignore them which would make me look naïve or afraid, neither of which will produce trust.

Think about your tendencies. What things might make you appear to be untrustworthy? Work on these things.

Time Utilization

In my book *The Process 2*, I explain how to use your time efficiently in building your business. That is more targeted for the newer business builder who is now putting a network marketing business into the mix of a busy life and needs to know the basics for accomplishing the work. In my first book *Live Full, Live Well* I teach Life Management concepts which help people be highly efficient in how they use time in general to create a life of higher joy, fulfillment, and success. Both of those resources would be valuable to you if you have not read them.

This section tackles time issues at a different level. The demands on your time and the challenges you have in balancing those demands grow exponentially larger as you begin to establish yourself as a leader and have a growing organization. In most cases emerging leaders must balance their existing career (people will still have a job even as they become a leader) and their other personal responsibilities, with building their business and leading others. As the network continues to grow, *it becomes essentially a full-time business while you are still part-time.* Since you have a limited amount of time to work your business, it's important to use your time wisely. Learning how to best utilize time is one of the biggest challenges a rising leader will face. It's imperative to learn how to be effective in working with your time because not only do you have more responsibility, but making time mistakes are often *interpreted* as character mistakes to others. For example, if you don't return a phone call because you are overwhelmed with work, the person who is waiting for your call will believe you don't care about them. You may not think this is fair, but it will be true. A leader cannot afford anything that reflects poorly on his/her character.

Learning how to best utilize time is one of the biggest challenges a rising leader will face.

As the organization expands its easy to spend your time simply reacting. Returning calls, responding to emails and direct messages, participating in meetings you don't initiate, and addressing other things that come at you are important aspects of serving your organization. These are often comfortable and fun and have a place in your productivity. However, these tend to be reactive activities. Leaders are *proactive*. Leaders know that living in reaction is a poor way to utilize time and results in a drastically lower level of productivity. Only through purposeful time utilization can you remain proactive when you have a growing network.

How much time do you currently dedicate per week to working in your business? How much of that time do YOU plan?

Protecting Your Time

Developing a successful business means you are a person who will do what you say you will do. Being this type of person, it is natural to expect others to be the same way. You likely have several people right now that say they are going to build the business. Given that you are already juggling a busy schedule it is reasonable to think to yourself that you need to focus on these people at this time, rather than looking for new people. This makes sense because if these people are serious and begin to truly build the business you will be busy with supporting their efforts and working alongside of them. The challenge is, that the laws of human nature and numbers would indicate that this won't be completely true. Some of the people who *say* they will build the business will not build the business. This is a lesson you have probably already learned. In leadership we have to remember that there is a second funnel.

The first funnel is the basic one. That is, if ten people have an identical need to create more income, on average two of those people will be ready to take action on this need. This is a *human nature* statistic that consistently holds true. The second funnel relates to the two people who take the step to get involved in the business. Since the first step to join the organization does not require much of a commitment, it is not a true indicator of what the person will do. Taking the action to build the business is the second funnel. The second funnel takes ten people who join and reveals the two who will actually take action to grow their business. As leaders we have to remember that regardless of our terrific support and training, we will sponsor ten builders to find two that will truly require an investment of our time. This will also hold true in the organization as you meet people who have been sponsored in depth that would need your level of knowledge and guidance.

Are they doing what they said they would do?

The best way to deal with this issue is to place *no expectation* on others. Believe in everyone's potential and let them know you believe in them but depend only on yourself and your personal efforts until you are *shown* that someone is truly serious about building their business. So how do you know? A simple rule of knowing who to allocate time for is: Are they doing what they said they would do? It doesn't matter what pace they are working, whether it is 3 hours per week or 20 hours per week, it only matters if they are doing what they said they would do. If they are, then you know that you have someone you will need to be available to help.

Consider the people you are most actively supporting. Are they doing what they said they would do?

Time Allocation

You never want to ignore anyone in your organization. *Everyone has value* and should feel welcome and supported regardless of their level of activity. You have to respect whatever someone is choosing to do in their life, whether you agree or not, because it is their life. In a network, you do life together with the people. Life is full of seasons which means you will be together during good times and times of struggle relative to all aspects of life and business. Having said this, you must spend the majority of your active time in the business with the people who are doing what they said they would do. As your organization grows you must become more efficient in how you support. Understanding and working within the "Pareto Principle" will help you greatly to do this. The "Pareto Principle" is commonly known as the 80/20 principle. Richard Koch in his book *The 80/20 Principle* describes it well when he says, "The 80/20 Principle states that there is an inbuilt imbalance between causes and results, inputs and outputs, and effort and reward. A good benchmark for this imbalance is provided by the 80/20 relationship: a typical pattern will show that 80% of the outputs result from 20% of the inputs; that 80% of the consequences flow from 20% of the causes; or that 80% of the results come from 20% of the effort."

> *"The 80/20 Principle states that there is an inbuilt imbalance between causes and results, inputs and outputs, and effort and reward."*
>
> RICHARD KOCH

It universally applies to your business in the following way: 20% of your activities will yield 80% of your results and 20% of the people will provide 80% of your success. Using these two applications in your business is crucial for any successful leader. The 20% of your activities means of *all the things* you can be doing, 20% will produce 80% of your business results. In networking this means volume of products/services moving to consumers. From a personal standpoint for you as the business builder, the 20% activities are sponsoring and servicing. Therefore 80% of your time should be spent in these activities. Since you are a leader, this can mean the sponsoring you are doing yourself or the time you invest in helping your organization sponsor. The more difficult time struggle has to do with the second aspect which is that 20% of your people will generate 80% of your volume. You must learn how to give your time to the 20% without ignoring the other 80% of the people who only produce 20% of your volume. This is where you must learn how to use leveraged activities to support the 80% group while you invest time in strengthening and growing the leadership capabilities of your 20% group. It is easy to get this backwards. Many leaders take years to grasp this concept on their own. Strengthen your strength. Support and empower the rest. The way you serve the other 80% is through activities such as conference calls, local events, websites, and email in a general sense. You will still spend some individual time with this part of the organization but with leveraged support in place it will not be as much of your time.

Who are the people in your organization who are currently in the 20% group?

Front Side Time

It is vital to understand that even if we have sponsored several people who are actively building the business, we must continue to talk to new prospects. I touched on why this is important in the previous section on protecting your time because a common mistake a new leader makes in the business is to stop sponsoring new people once they have some true builders in place. There is a tendency to want to manage the people that you have sponsored and only work with them and their prospects. You have to recognize that the minute you stop actively recruiting new builders and customers you have placed the growth potential of the organization completely in the hands of others. You will no longer be a part of setting the pace of your business. Instead the organization will now dictate how fast your business can grow. Until you have reached some of your larger goals, you must always be a part of setting the pace. This is a lead by example business. The builders in your organization are always watching what you do and continued sponsoring sets the example for them. If you slow your sponsoring activities, it will not be long before your organization slows its sponsoring activities. They are simply duplicating what you are doing.

You have to recognize that the minute you stop actively recruiting new builders and customers you have placed the growth potential of the organization completely in the hands of others.

Set aside time each day to talk to new prospects. I call this the *front side* of the business. One of the great things that comes with the success that has positioned you to lead, is *your credibility has grown along with your success and your longevity in the business*, and sponsoring becomes easier. This means you will not need the same amount of time to sponsor new people that you needed in the early stages of building your business. However you will need to be purposeful in staying in the front side activities because you could easily spend the day just working in the organization. The way to make sure this happens is to put your front side activities *first* in your schedule. Treat this time like an appointment with yourself. When you are working in this time, do not take incoming calls or emails that are not part of your front side work, just like you would if you were in an appointment.

There *will* be times when the demands on you from your builders for "productive" time take all of your time. Productive time is when you are doing meetings and conference calls in the organization that are related to growing the business. This will be a natural point where you slow your sponsoring activities temporarily. But don't completely stop, unless of course you have achieved your goals!

Given your current organization activity, how much time will you invest in front side activities per day?

Communicating with the Network

Communicating with the network is a practical part of your time utilization as a leader. There are lots of aspects to this. I'll only cover some of the basic ones that are helpful as this is an important part of 80/20 time allocation.

Email: Email is an excellent tool to share fact based information as well as answer questions that are not urgent. Since your organization is made up of customers and business builders, you should have separate lists for each. I honor leadership within the organization, so I create a business builder list of the people I directly work with and have recruited. This is who I send business related emails to such as tips, event announcements, and stories of interest. They can then send this on to the members of their teams. I only include people from their teams in this email list if the leader asks me to because I am respectful of their position and they need to be the *point person* for their teams. The customer email list is all the customers I serve and the same business builder group because they too are customers. I send only customer based information to this group. Once again, the builders can then decide if they would like to send the information on to their customer groups. Two things that should never go through email are time sensitive things or issues that are emotionally charged.

Text: Texting is an excellent time utilization tool. In leadership, it's an excellent way to maintain connectivity and do *quick touches*. A quick touch is simply a short message to encourage and ask if there is anything you can do to help. WhatsApp, Facebook Messenger, Skype and a host of other instant messaging tools all do the same thing. For example, let's suppose there is a situation that has arisen that you need to address with a few of your key leaders. A quick message asking if they can do a conference call at a specific time of day, reduces the need to make phone calls in order to have a phone call. Most of your leaders are busy and a call is not as efficient in this case as an instant message.

Social networks: Social networking platforms, like Facebook, are also excellent communicating tools for the entire community. There are new platforms being introduced to the market all the time-take your pick. You can set these up easily by creating a private group and inviting members into this. This gives you a very effective platform to promote events and share ideas, stories, and tips for the organization. It's also a great place to recognize and praise people in the organization. The other component this serves is the feeling of belonging and connection for the network. It's a place where the network can interact and share with each other that creates cohesiveness and reduces the amount of questions and support that you have to provide because the network is also supporting each other. One important thing to note, is be careful not to *over post*. The more people hear one voice the less impact it has.

Open Webinars and Conference Calls: These are excellent leveraged platforms for teaching and recognition. Today's technology makes these inexpensive to do, and easy for everyone to access. They serve as events where someone can participate from wherever they are, as opposed to the limitations of relying purely on a physical meeting culture. By doing these in an open and interactive way, you are able to teach and share in an open forum where one person can ask a question, but all are able to benefit from the answers.

All of these tools serve as a means to leverage your time such that you can consistently reach all corners of the network regardless of where the people are geographically. Leaders will need to use all these mechanisms to serve the organization and stay in touch and at the same time, it allows the leader great flexibility in their own time use. Nothing is better than a live conversation with someone but in order to preserve the time you need to have live conversations with the right people about the right things, it is vital that you employ all the above mechanisms to best serve the organization as a whole.

How are you currently using these tools to support the network and what can you do to improve your effectiveness?

Working ON versus Working IN

Many years ago Michael Gerber wrote an excellent book called the E-Myth. In this book he talks about how many entrepreneurs fail because as their business grows they spend less and less time working in the business and more time working on the business. What he is describing is particularly relevant to the smaller entrepreneur who begins a business because they enjoy, and are skilled in, the thing they are doing. Let's say, for example, they like to make children's clothes. As a side business, they start making children's clothes and then on weekends they go to craft shows and sell them. Over time they begin to generate enough income that they believe they can earn a full time living in the children's clothes business so they leave their job to pursue the dream of working for themselves. They are now in the business of making and selling children's clothes full time. They open up a store front where they sell the clothes. However, they now have a lot more to do than just make and sell children's clothes don't they? Making and selling children's clothes is what produces the revenue that leads to their profit which provides their income. However, they now have an entirely new set of responsibilities that are vital to keeping their business running. They have to book-keep, forecast, manage the store and its inventory, manage dealing with the suppliers, deal with the tax and regulatory environment of running a business, eventually hire employees, pay them, and on and on. These are mostly working *on* the business activities. Before long, this small entrepreneur is spending so much time working on the business and usually in areas that are not their strengths (which is making and selling the clothes) that they are no longer efficiently doing the most important activity which is working *in* the business. Gerber states in his book that "the business that was supposed to free him from the limitations of working for somebody else, actually *enslaves* him. Suddenly the job he knew how to do so well becomes one job he knows how to do *plus a dozen others he doesn't know how to do at all.*"*

This book was written in 1986 which was a different time, in terms of technology, than today. This same entrepreneur can more easily outsource this today as well as decide to sell by the internet instead of have the costs of a storefront. But the equation won't change. Either way, there will be many aspects of running the business than just making and selling the clothes. Too much time working on a business instead of in a business will lead to its failing.

> *"The business that was supposed to free him from the limitations of working for somebody else, actually enslaves him. Suddenly the job he knew how to do so well becomes one job he knows how to do plus a dozen others he doesn't know how to do at all."*
>
> MICHAEL GERBER

So how does this relate to you? Because of the nature of network marketing, you don't have to work too much on the business. The company does most of this. You just have to focus on working the process, and training, coaching, and mentoring others as the organization grows. *You can spend most of your time working in the business.* But let's be real. You are an entrepreneur. The longer you are in the business the more you will have creative ideas about how the business can be made more successful. You will have ideas about tools that you believe would be beneficial. You will think about ways to attract new people to your teams. You will be looking ahead to when is a good time to introduce a new promotion. I know how this feels, because my mind is constantly working on new ideas. When you care deeply about helping people succeed, it's difficult to turn off your brain! You want to keep things fresh from a forward thinking perspective because people need to have new things to renew their excitement. You will constantly be brainstorming. This is good and you *should* do it. You just have to be careful not to spend too much time working on the business, especially early in the growth of your organization. Until you have built an organization that is financially sustaining you at a comfortable level, you should spend little to no time working on the business. Stay in it. Keep working the wheel that is already round!

As a leader there will be times when you *will* be working on the business, so it is important to understand timing as it relates to significant projects. Let's say you have a brainstorm for a program that you believe will fuel new growth. Assess first what is going on currently in the network. If they are in the midst of growth then this is not the time to introduce a new idea. Refine it and prepare it during the current growth phase and when things begin to slow and pull-back, then you have the ideal time to refresh the energy by introducing the new program or idea. So how do you do this the right way? Do you just announce a big webinar or meeting or conference call and then lay out your great idea? Absolutely not.

Regardless of how good the idea is, you are dealing with human beings and the majority of people are resistant to any kind of change at first. The thing to do is consult your top leadership first and let them know you have an idea you would like their input on. Give your leadership the opportunity to be part of creating the program. They will automatically have buy-in if they have a role in the program. Then you will have a unified group of leaders driving the new idea into the organization and a much higher probability of success with the new idea.

Do you have ideas now for tools and programs? If so, make note of them in your journal and assess the current environment of the organization. Continue to refine the idea in your journal as you assess the timing and climate.

Financial Prudence

Many people who achieve significant success in networking are in a new situation. They come from a situation of working for someone to living life as an entrepreneur. This means that they need to have a new understanding of managing financial resources and handling taxes the proper way. I know how important this is because in my early years in the industry I made some huge financial mistakes that took me years to recover from.

Unless you are a financial advisor or tax professional it's not your place to give advice in this area, just as it's not my place either. However taking care of your finances is important for you as a leader. Consult the tax laws for your country to understand when income taxes are due and what types of deductions you are eligible to take from your expenses. A good rule of thumb is to take a portion of your commission check that is equal to what taxes you would owe on this income and place it in a separate bank account that you do not touch for personal use. Then, at whatever scheduled date your country requires, pay your taxes from this account. Also, set up a simple system to keep track of your expenses so you can deduct them in the way your tax laws allow. Keep all of your receipts and credit card statements in one place and organize them at least monthly to keep it manageable. A separate bank account for your business is also a good idea and may be required depending on where you live.

Be careful not to spend money today based on your future business projections.

Once you have paid all of your taxes for the year, if you have any money left in the tax account, then you can choose to take this money for personal use, or leave it to begin the new tax year. If you need a deeper understanding consult with a tax professional. Once you have your financial ship in order, you can share what you do with the rising leaders in your network (not as advice, only as example). Also, be careful not to spend money today based on your future business projections.

It is a common mistake as the network is growing to begin to dramatically increase your standard of living. This is a business. There will be seasons of growth and seasons of challenge. Be smart about how you build your life. Always have resources set aside that you don't need. Keep your monthly obligations low. Financial stress is an attitude killer. I have seen way too many people in my career buy the big house and the fancy cars before they built a solid financial base only to put themselves in a troubled position. The nice things will come if that's what you want, but don't look at your network as it grows and start banking on income you haven't earned yet.

Do you have a system for managing your finances?

Specifically what makes them want to?

I mentioned earlier that leadership in a network marketing organization is the purest form of leadership because you are leading people who are not required to follow you. They are volunteers working for their own purposes. There is no formal consequence should they choose to ignore you and do their own thing as soon as you sponsor them. They have to want to follow you. John Maxwell refers to this as gaining permission. In his book *The 5 Levels of Leadership* he says "Trust is the foundation of permission. If you have integrity with people, you develop trust. The more trust you develop, the stronger the relationship becomes. The better the relationship, the greater the potential for a leader to gain permission to lead. It's a building process that takes time, energy, and intentionality."*

I talked at length earlier about how the degree of your credibility determines the degree to which someone would follow you, and that the purposeful application of this credibility results in the level of your influence. Now it's important to focus on the exact things that produce the trust that is the true beginning of someone wanting to follow you. There are many things that can play a part in this, some of which are driven by the actual character traits of the leader, but the following five are the most important, and fortunately they are easy to do.

1. **Be effective in the core competencies:** The core competencies are the fundamental steps in the process (approach, information, follow up, customer service, and training a new builder). It must be evident that you are good in these.

2. **Know your company and be a resource for accurate information:** You need to know all about the company itself (The story of its genesis, the key players, and the points of difference in the market place that make it unique and attractive). You also need to know where to find important information, but you don't *need* to know it all. You only need to know where to find the information. No one expects you to know every tiny detail of everything.

3. **Have integrity and be authentic:** If this is questioned even a little bit, trust cannot be built to the level needed to establish the credibility that produces influence.

4. **Be responsive and available:** Return phone calls, emails, texts, and direct messages in a timely manner. The definition of a timely manner is up to you to decide, but I will tell you what I do. I return calls as soon as I can possibly do it and, as a rule, in the same day (unless I have made it known I am traveling or on vacation). The same is true of texts and direct messages. I base the speed of my response to emails on the nature of the email, and with any actionable email it will be as soon as possible. I return all calls. *Available* means showing up to help when someone needs it. If you are in the organization I serve and you need help with a prospect or to meet a new member, or to do a three-way call, a meeting, or you need some coaching, all you have to do is ask and I will do it if I can.

5. **Set a good example:** Example is a big topic and can represent lots of things but for this specific scenario there are three things that matter most and they are simple:

    - Use all the products or services you can from your company and make sure they are visible in your home where appropriate.
    - Treat people well. You already know what I mean but I will say it again. Be nice, honest and respectful.
    - Demonstrate a strong work ethic. The organization needs to see you are actively working in some way, for several reasons, but for the want to concept, it's about doing the work they are doing. In addition to them knowing you are doing the work too, it helps them trust you to know what they are experiencing as they work, and allows your input to be valued.

Consider these five things. How are you doing in each area? Should the organization want to follow you right now?

Ask the Right Questions

The people in your organization are working for themselves. As such, they will not appreciate questions like "What are you doing?" or "What have you done today?" or "How many calls have you made today?" unless they are asked in the right way at the right time. In general, any question that elicits the feeling of having to answer to someone else will not be well received (unless an accountability format has been mutually agreed upon). As a network marketing leader it is your role to serve your people in growing, developing, and succeeding, not to manage them. Therefore, the questions you ask need to be pointed in this direction.

You really don't need to ask people what they have been doing anyway. You have the ability to track their progress through technology in a variety of ways. You can see if they are sponsoring, see their business volume, see how well they are retaining people, and see if there is duplication in their organization. Instead of asking what they are doing, it is better to ask what is keeping them from making progress and how you can help, or what you can do to serve the success they are having. Here are some of the types of questions you can ask:

Are there any new questions you have or that you have been asked that you need help with?

What can I help you with?

Is there anything I can help you with?

Who are you talking to that I can help you with?

What can I do for you?

What are you struggling with?

How are you feeling about things?

I suggest you make up some of your own questions. These are just some easy examples to use that open the conversation. What? How? Who? These are relatively open ended questions that allow them to share openly and provide you with the ability to ask the next important question. Once you are in a discussion and they know you are communicating from a helpful perspective, then you can ask a more pointed question like "how many people did you talk to?" or "what are you saying when you talk to someone?" because the question is now in the context of helping them.

What? How? Who? These are relatively open ended questions that allow them to share openly and provide you with the ability to ask the next important question.

One of the things you have to keep in mind is that many of the people you sponsor, especially those deeper in the organization, do not truly understand that you are open to help them and answer questions when they need it. They are not accustomed to this in the rest of their working lives, where bureaucracy and position often minimize accessibility to those higher in the organization. The bottom line is that they are not used to the awesome level of support you will provide them. Often someone will be struggling and don't feel that they can call you about it. By reaching out and touching them in a nice open helpful way, they are more likely to open up with you and give you an opportunity to help them. When you do this the right way, it further demonstrates to them how much better it is to work in a networking marketing organization than a bureaucratic structure.

It's also important for you to ask yourself the right questions. It doesn't matter who you are or at what level you are in your success. You are a human being and we humans have struggles and difficulties. When things are going well and you don't feel any struggle ask yourself these kinds of questions, "What can I do better?" "What can I work on?" What do I want to learn?" "What do I want to master?" "What can I do to serve the organization better?" When you are having difficult times there is a tendency for all of us to focus on the problem. Leaders ask this simple question first, "What can I do?" Then they follow it up with "What will I do?" These questions, with the emphasis on "can" or "will" are empowering questions of certainty. You know you will get through whatever it is, that's what leaders do, so focus purely on doing it, not on the problem itself.

What are the questions you will ask to those you lead?

Lead Them Where They Are

The long term business builders in your organization will tend to fall into three categories. The first are the people whose income needs are met by achieving $300-500 per month. This will be around 80% of your working community. The second are those who achieve $1000 plus per month which will be about 15% of the community, and the third category will be those who develop a full-time income which will comprise about 5% of the community (this has a different meaning depending on the person. It could be $60,000 a year or $200,000 or more).

There will often be people who believe they want to be in a certain category and then as time goes on they change their aspirations. The most important thing to understand is that as a leader your focus is on helping each person accomplish what's important to *them*. This can be a challenge for a leader because you can see what someone is capable of, you know what's possible for them, and you are also working to expand your business. As is often the result, the greatest failure in leadership is with the 80% group. We must always remember the adage espoused by the late renowned motivational guru Zig Ziglar that "you can have everything in life you want, if you will just help enough other people get what they want."*

Given that the 80% group is the highest percentage of your business building community, it is natural that this *could* be the biggest challenge. But it doesn't have to be. Instead, it can be the easiest portion of the community to support. The thing to recognize is the 80% group is accomplishing exactly what they want to accomplish financially, but there is more to it than just money for this group. Because the money part is relatively small in the big picture, these same people could achieve this in many other ways in their lives. So, while the money is important, the *experience* is equally important. The business needs to be enjoyable for them. They need to feel valued and appreciated. They like to be involved in the community both socially and from the standpoint of the spirit and purpose of the community. To pressure them to do more will drive them away. This is why I see the biggest failure in this area. Overzealous leaders push these people when they don't want to be pushed. You should expose them to what is possible and encourage them, but most importantly, you should *love* them. Think of it this way… love them or they will leave. It's that simple. And this group is easy to love. Once they know what to do they typically demand very little of your working time and are easily served through good time allocation skills. Only good things come from treating this group with the respect they deserve. Many times, just by the sheer numbers that this group aggregately touches, a 15% person or a 5% person will be sponsored. Now you have a new major builder from a group without major aspirations. There will also be times when changes in life or sudden inspiration causes a person from this group to decide to move forward and pursue a higher level of success. When this happens, since you have always been supportive and shown appreciation, they will be ready to work with you to make this move in their business, as opposed to looking for another company to work with. Sometimes, their own level of personal development leads to a higher belief in themselves and they decide that they want to go higher. Again, this is based solely on *their decision*. There are countless examples of someone who started in the industry to make a little extra money and wound up building a large organization. This will happen as it's supposed to if you love your people.

Love them or they will leave.

The 15% group is also a place where it can be easy to try to push them to do more. After all, $1000-2000 per month is a strong business and demonstrates that they can absolutely build bigger if they want to. You have to remember *it is about them, not what you want for them*. Some will decide to go further and others will be happy to stay in this range and earn this same income for years to come. The same ideals are in place here that work for the 80% group.

If you attempt to control them they will break away from you completely.

The 5% group represents an entirely different challenge. These are the ones that have truly embraced entrepreneurship. These are your leaders and rising leaders. In essence, once they have achieved a full time level of success, they are *running their own show*, or will be very soon. They will have all kinds of ideas about how they want to see their business develop for the future. Some of their ideas you will agree with and some you won't. Do not try to control them. They are successful in the business at a significant level. You want to continue to have a great working relationship with them. If you attempt to control them they will break away from you completely and it will cause conflict that is unnecessary. Here is a simple way to think about this: *Let them fly*. You worked a long time to help them be able to fly high without you. Don't reach up now and try to hold them down. They will resent you for it. Instead, acknowledge their achievements, ask them how you can support them, and collaborate with them as much as possible, but give them the respect they have earned. If they have an idea, brainstorm it with them and offer your input and experience, but keep your heart in the place of serving them and you will have a prosperous relationship into the future and a lot of fun.

In my early years of developing myself as a leader, I had significant failures in all three groups. I pushed some in the 80% and 15% groups when I shouldn't have. I tried to over-control some in the 5% group instead of acknowledging their accomplishments and treating them as peers. The result? I lost those people permanently. Many went on to have success in other organizations where the leadership served them better than I did. Lead them and serve them where they are. Love them and appreciate them. And they will be with you for a long time.

Who are your 80%, your 15% and your 5% and how will you go forward and serve them?

Patient Frustration

Patient frustration seems like an oxymoron doesn't it? Much like jumbo shrimp! Linguistically it is certainly true, but in the context of leadership it is a practiced art that is important. Let's start with frustration. Who likes frustration? On the surface frustration seems like a negative thing because it typically produces negative emotions. But what does it really mean to be frustrated? Dictionary.com defines frustration as: a feeling of dissatisfaction, often accompanied by anxiety or depression, resulting from unfulfilled needs or unresolved problems. From my experience, frustration happens when something isn't going the way I want it to. We can probably agree on this. What makes frustration possible is caring and this is precisely why I consider frustration a good thing. If something you don't care about doesn't work out, so what? You don't worry about it or give it a second thought-after all who cares? Frustration is really about caring that something is not going as you expect or want. Networking leaders are doers. They are big thinkers that make things happen. They make things happen through their own effort and by working with and serving others who are working toward what they care about. By the very nature of the work, this means there will be frustration. *All* things of value produce enormous frustration at times. Growing and leading a network has tremendous value so it's naturally going to produce times of frustration. This frustration is more than worth it. It's vital. If you're not experiencing some level of frustration on a consistent basis, you are either *not trying* to accomplish anything or you are on an incredible lucky streak that won't last!

What makes frustration possible is caring and this is precisely why I consider frustration a good thing.

I want you to have frustration. And I want you to have lots of it. Because I know this means you care deeply and you are working hard to build something of huge value. The lifestyle fruits of leading a large network are better than most every other income vehicle in the world, but it will take some frustration to create it. You would have frustration in any income vehicle. You have probably had a great deal of frustration in your current or previous job or business (without the lifestyle benefits of network marketing). So now that you are clear that having some frustration represents something positive-*immensely positive*-let's talk about its necessary partner; patience.

All things of value produce enormous frustration at times.

I believe patience is a struggle for all of us. Human beings want what they want, and they want it yesterday! Is a baby patient? I don't think so. The minute a baby is hungry or has a wet diaper, you know about it don't you? The longer it takes for you to address the hunger or the diaper, the louder the baby will scream. That baby is alive and well in all of us. We learn to deal with our impatience in a socially acceptable way, but that doesn't mean we are any more patient! Being an entrepreneur, which is what you and I are, requires patience. We know that nothing of value happens overnight, but we don't have to like it. Your patience is tested in multiple ways as you grow your organization. The first area in which you need to practice patience is in your own skill development. We all have our strengths and weaknesses when it comes to working the process, so regardless of our business experience in life, we will have a learning curve. You cannot be good at something until have worked through the period of time where you aren't so good. The fact that you are an aspiring leader means you have become very good in enough areas of the process to off-set the areas where you are not as strong.

Leadership skills are an entirely new arena. The competencies that put you in a position to lead are *not the same ones you will need to effectively lead*. This will require you to be patient with yourself while you learn new skills. It will take time to master the time utilization skills needed at the leadership level. It will take practice to become effective in coaching, empowering, inspiring, and communicating on a larger scale. This will frustrate you so you will need to be patient. You'll make mistakes-and that's okay, it's a big part of how you learn. Legendary basketball coach John Wooden put a great light on the value of mistakes when he said "The person who is afraid to risk failure seldom has to face success. I expected my players to make mistakes as long as they were mistakes of commission. A mistake of commission happens when you are doing what should be done but don't get the results you want...the team that makes the most mistakes usually wins, if those mistakes aren't careless."*

Personal development is another area that requires patience and consistent effort. For example, you will discover tendencies and habits that you have acquired through your life that aren't helpful. You will find areas of weakness that negatively impact your ability to use your strengths. This is inherent in the process of personal growth. Once you recognize them, you will prefer to change them immediately, but despite your best intentions it won't happen right away. It is true that old habits die hard. You will have to purposefully and patiently persevere through the process of growth until you overcome the issue. Here's a simple example to demonstrate the point. Some time ago I had a total knee replacement. I had completely worn out my knee through years of sports. Since my knee had been worn out for several years, and I had delayed the surgery as long as possible, I had developed a habit of stepping down off a curb or step in a certain way in order to protect myself from pain. For years I would step down with my bad leg because bending it to step down with the other leg would cause me discomfort. Once the joint was replaced, that changed. I now have the task of protecting the new knee so that the replacement lasts as long as possible. Stepping down with the reconstructed leg causes the bones of the lower leg to crash into the new knee because of the force of gravity. This is okay normally because our body has cartilage to protect the bones. However, I don't have any cartilage so this would cause the new joint to wear out faster. Once I learned about this I began the process of *learning* to step down with the other leg. You would think this would have been easy to do. After all, it was simply stepping down off a curb. Something

I have been doing since I was two years old! But for several years I had been training myself into the habit of always stepping down a certain way. I never had to think about it. I just did it. So what did I naturally do? Step down with the wrong leg! For the first month, I would automatically step off the curb with the wrong leg. Then I would realize what I just did, go back up on the curb, and step down with the right leg. I'm sure I looked quite strange as I was constantly stepping off a curb, turning around, going back on the curb, and stepping down again. It was a little frustrating. After a few months I got to the point where it became almost natural to step down with the right leg. I still had to think about it every now and then but the learning was almost complete. This was after two months of conscious effort. This is how personal development works when creating new habits and tendencies. You will have to feel silly at times and it will frustrate you, but if you stay patient you will grow.

You will have to feel silly at times and it will frustrate you, but if you stay patient you will grow.

The next area you will need to practice patience is with the people you are working with and leading. More people than not will frustrate you. They won't be as committed as you, they won't do what you show them to do, and they won't go as fast as you know they can go. They will think they know better than you even though they are relatively new and you clearly know what to do. You have to be patient with them. They are not running your race. My wife Melanie taught me this concept many years ago when I was pushing her to do something the way I would want it done and at the speed I would want it done. She looked at me and said "Todd I am not running YOUR race." That lesson has served me well. They have to go through their own learning curve and their own situations. Yes, you want it for them, but it just takes people their own time in order to really "get it." You have to be accepting and never let them see your frustration. *Never let them see your impatience.* They will construe this as you wanting them to do it for YOU. You cannot allow this to happen if you want to maintain your leadership influence with them. They must always believe that you have their best interest at heart (remember you must lead them where THEY are).

The final area that you will need patience is with the growth rate of the organization. You will rarely be satisfied with this *even in times of terrific growth.* It's just the nature of an entrepreneur to want it to go faster than it's going regardless of how fast it is going! Get used to this. The bigger the organization grows the less ability you have to increase it through your own actions day to day. It's just basic mathematics. Your personal productivity is a smaller percentage of the organization as it gets larger. You will need patience to do the work necessary to lead it to higher levels because at this point your growth is almost entirely based on everyone else's actions.

Where, and with whom, do you need to demonstrate the most patience in your business currently?

Praise Power

Praise is a powerful tool if you know how to use it properly. As leaders, we must understand that the people we are working with are rarely getting praised in their lives whether at their workplace or outside of their work. If the people in the world received as much praise as they do criticism, the world would be a much happier place. Unfortunately this is not the case. It's normal to be told when you are doing something wrong isn't it? Now think about this: how often are YOU praised? Probably not very much, and you are someone who is doing a lot of good things for a lot of people!

Author and leadership expert Ken Blanchard refers to praise as "catching people doing something right." I love this concept because as leaders we *want* to catch people doing something right! And then *let them know*. Blanchard gives us insight into why we want to do this when he says "Catching people doing things right provides satisfaction and motivates performance."* This is exactly what you want in your organization isn't it? Satisfied people who are motivated to perform! When offering praise, it's important to consider the things you value and that you would want the organization doing. Recognize that the things you praise are likely to be repeated so praise what you would like to see repeated. It is also important to know exactly how to deliver praise in the most effective way. Here are some guidelines for excellent praise:

1) **Be specific:** Telling someone "good job" is not specific enough. You need to tell someone *exactly* what it is that they did well. How can someone repeat a good job? They need to know precisely what made it a good job and was worthy of praise.

2) **Do it now:** Praise someone as quickly as you can. Time is of the essence. If they did something well today then today is the time to tell them. *Reinforce the behavior quickly and they will do more of it faster.* If you wait two weeks or a month to praise an act, too much time has elapsed and the impact will be lost.

3) **Be sincere:** It needs to be a real thing. If you are construed as praising something that is not true or not as valuable as you are portraying it to be, this will have the opposite effect. It will have the person questioning your integrity as well as the merit of the thing you are praising.

4) **Praise publicly:** The best praise is in front of others in the business. I know some people immediately push back on this one and say that it embarrasses them to be praised in front of others-especially those who are more introverted. Being an introvert myself, I can tell you that there is some truth to this. I can also tell you that the 10 seconds of embarrassment is well worth it when compared to the *entire day* of feeling good because of being praised in front of others. Their chest will stick out a little more and their head will be held a little higher the rest of the day. They will be more energized and effective in their work. So go ahead and embarrass them a little. *They will love it.* If there is not the opportunity to immediately praise in front of others then praise in the private moment, and the next time there is an appropriate setting, perhaps a conference call or a meeting, praise them again for the sake of the public. You can also praise in a group social networking site. The multiplying effect of praising in public is that others in the network will hear it and recognize what was done to earn the praise. Since everyone likes praise, you will likely have more people who will do the thing that was praised!

5) **Impact:** If the action that was taken had a positive impact on you as the leader make sure you communicate what kind of impact it had. Let them know exactly how what they did was helpful or beneficial. This would be true also if it benefitted the organization as a whole.

Make praise a habit. Be purposeful in finding out what people are doing that is good and let them know you have noticed.

Who can you praise today?

Keep your Old Shoes

You are becoming or already are a leader. This means that you have worked through countless personal struggles, doubts, mistakes, and life situations, in addition to what you went through to start your business and begin to succeed. You had countless people tell you that you were crazy, stupid, a dreamer, or foolish. You had some of the people closest to you tell you no and that what you are doing will never work. They told you that you are wasting your time. Metaphorically, you began the business in a beat up pair of shoes that got completely worn out as you grew your organization. You were then able to afford some newer and better looking shoes. At that point, not as many people doubted you or your business. Instead they began to respect you and in many cases admit that you knew what you were doing after all. The process got easier and easier for you. You became confident. Your self-doubts shrunk. Sure you still have your moments because you are human, but not like when you started.

Never forget where you came from or what you went through to become successful.

My advice to you is to keep those old shoes. The people you are working with are wearing their version of the shoes you started in. You can never forget where you came from or what you went through to become successful. Your organization only sees you now in your new shoes. You look confident. You look successful. You seem to know all the right things to do. They need to believe that they can someday wear the kind of shoes you are wearing now. In order for you to help them believe this, you need to pull out your old shoes and tell them about them.

I consistently share stories about the awful things my family and friends said to me. I talk about how hard making an initial contact was for me. I talk about my horrifying experiences when I first had to stand in front of people and do a presentation. I talk about the tiny apartment I started in, how I had to do one-on-one meetings with a crying baby in my arms, about the countless times I showed up to do an in-home presentation for someone in the downline and no one showed up, about wondering how I would pay the bills. Doubts, fears, tears, heart-breaks, mistakes, rough times…I could write an entire book on my old shoes!

Your organization needs to know you have been in your version of their shoes. That you kept walking in those shoes regardless of what you faced, and that this is what led to you getting to the new shoes you wear now. This helps them connect to where you've come from. Never play down your old shoes. Show them as much as possible!

What are some of the lessons from your old shoes?

Be a CEEO

CEO stands for Chief Executive Officer. This is usually the highest formal leadership position that can be achieved in a corporation. In your networking business, you want to be the CEEO: The Chief Encouragement and Empathy Officer.

Encouragement is "the oxygen of the soul" (I first saw this in a John Maxwell book, but I'm not certain who first said this). This is such a true statement. Think about how it makes you feel when someone encourages you. It's like a breath of fresh air. I believe this is because most people are not receiving much encouragement in their lives. They tend to receive criticism, correction, advice, and the rare compliment, but not encouragement. Encouragement is when someone shares with you that you are on the right path, that you can do it, that you have what it takes, that they believe in you. How valuable is this? It's as valuable to your pursuits in life as oxygen is to your body. When you truly encourage someone, they feel good. They feel like you know what they are trying to do and that you have faith that they can.

Empathy is often a partner with encouragement. Encouragement is a good thing at any time, but it has the most value when someone is struggling. Empathy is shown when you communicate that you really understand what someone is going through. Only when you display empathy, can your encouragement and your guidance have real meaning. When someone who doesn't really understand what you are going through tells you that you can do it, it doesn't ring true because it has no foundation in YOUR reality. I talked about the importance of interpersonal communication skills earlier and specifically mentioned the value of listening. Listening is the basis for being effective in empathic communication. You cannot exhibit empathy without first being an excellent listener. Why is this so? Because empathy is about recognizing and acknowledging how someone is feeling in a situation. You have to listen in a deep way to discern this. Then you need the empathic skill to work through the situation with them. The late Stephen Covey in his book the Seven Habits of Highly Effective People, has an entire chapter devoted to "Seek first to understand, then to be understood." This is the foundation of empathic communication. Here are some excerpts from Covey that encapsulate the value of learning this important leadership skill:

"Comparatively few people have had any training in listening at all. And, for the most part, their training has been in the personality ethic of technique, truncated from the character base and the relationship absolutely vital to authentic understanding of another person. If you want to interact effectively with me-your spouse, your child, your neighbor, your boss, your coworker, your friend-you first need to understand me. And you can't do that with technique alone…The real key to your influence with me is your example, your actual conduct. Your example flows naturally out of your character, or the kind of person you truly are…It is evident in how I actually experience you…You have to build the skills of empathic listening on a base of character that inspires openness and trust."*-Stephen Covey

The more empathy you can convey the more trust you will build with the people you are working with. You know how important trust is because we have talked about it. What's important to recognize is that the more trusted you are, the more effective your empathy. It starts with the trust you build as you grow your character perception prior to having permission to lead. Once you are in the position to lead, meaning the foundation of trust has been built, now the use of empathy massively grows the trust. It's a natural, powerful cycle. Empathic communication is a big topic and is one I suggest you study, so for now here are a few tips you can use to begin to become effective in communicating with empathy:

1) Listen with full attention: This means total focus. Make the other person feel as if they are the most important person in the world at this moment. Don't interrupt, don't break eye contact, and don't do anything that might indicate that you are not giving them your full attention. You are literally studying every aspect of them as they talk. Their words, their body language, their tone of voice and pace of conversation, their facial expressions, everything about how they are speaking and what they are feeling.

2) Let them know that you are trying to understand: You cannot make any assumptions during the conversation. You must continually ask clarifying questions like "what do you mean by that?" or "Are you saying…?" This allows them to express the true issue, and at the same time demonstrates that you care enough to want to know. Then you describe what you think you heard them say and you put this in the context of both the facts of the situation and the feelings you perceive they are expressing.

3) Communicate from a place of perception: As they are sharing with you it will become clearer to you what the true issue is. You have to express this back to them in terms of your perception, not in terms of absolutes. Don't say things like "You are…" because now you are labeling them and assuming based on what you are interpreting. Instead use phrases like "It appears to me that you are" "It seems to me that you are" "what I think I'm hearing is…is this right?" In this way you are showing that you aren't certain and inviting them to clarify or confirm. Otherwise they will feel judged or worse, not listened to.

4) Avoid saying these things:

- a) I know how you feel: You might understand how someone could feel a certain way, but regardless of your depth of experience you do not know how THEY feel. They are a unique individual with their own set of feelings and life experiences. If you say this they might become defensive and you will have broken the bond you are building.

- b) You shouldn't let that bother you: You have a lot of experience and have weathered many storms in your life and business. You will hear things that you think are ridiculous to even *be* an issue. You cannot say so. If you do you have minimized their struggle and they will feel badly about it. Remember that one person's mountain is another's speed bump.

c) Oh, that's nothing, let me tell you about a time when I…: In the same vein as the previous statement, you have likely been through your own difficult things. If you pull one of your stories out at this moment it will make them feel small, and you have now made the discussion about YOU and your heroics. This is a major rapport breaker and they will not trust that they can come to you with challenges because how could you understand their little problems when you have overcome such big problems? There is a place for you to inspire through your past victories, but at the moment they are sharing is not the time.

d) Here's what you should do: In an empathic conversation it is not your role to give advice. If you invest in the conversation deeply there will be a time to share your ideas fully. But first you have to let them know you completely understand what they are going through. As you will see in the coaching section, you would then ask them what they think they should do and help them work through their own solutions. Only give advice when you are asked for it.

The power to being a CEEO is that you build a large amount of emotional equity with the people you lead. You have invested in them as a human being and they are certain that you care about them. You understand them and they know and feel it. You are now one of the few people in their life that they believe really understands them. When you combine this with your success in the business it positions you to lead them in a powerful way. Because when you coach and mentor them, they will be confident that what you are saying is in *their* best interest and when you encourage them and share why you believe in them, they will begin to believe more in themselves.

How are you displaying empathy? How often do you provide true encouragement? How will you develop these areas in your leadership?

It's Not About Motivating

I often hear people who are working to build a network refer to someone who is not taking action as being unmotivated. You might have thought or said this yourself. But guess what? There are NO unmotivated people. Every single human being is motivated. The question is, for what are they motivated? It is never your job to motivate someone since they are already motivated. Your job is to find out what they are motivated by and empower and inspire them to move forward. The key thing here is *what is important to them*.

Your first task is to discover what they truly want and why they want it. This helps you to help them and it strengthens the relationship because they begin to believe that you care about them. Most people in their lives are not asking them what is truly important and they definitely aren't investing themselves in helping them get it. YOU ARE. You are distinguishing yourself as a voice that is *for* them.

Once you understand what truly matters to them you can then help them see how the steps you are teaching them will put them on the path to achieving the thing that they want. This connection of the actions to their goals is essential in having them take action. Essentially you are aligning their motivator with *the process*. This is a key belief they must develop. If they don't believe the process, that each tiny step will help them achieve what matters to them, they will not take action. Remember, you have to put your old shoes back on and reflect on what it felt like to come home from work tired and drained from a day of working for someone else, and then sit down and invest what little energy you have left in the day to build your network. High belief in the process of building will excite them and energize them to take action at the end of a work day. You are working with their *leftover energy* from the day. You have to help them see that it's just as important to invest these few hours per night in *themselves and their dreams* as the entire day they gave to someone else's dream that simply pays the bills temporarily but doesn't take them much closer to what they really want out of life. *Belief* in the process as the path to their success *inspires* them.

Another source of inspiration is the sharing of stories. I have already mentioned that sharing your past challenges and struggles is a way for them to understand that they CAN grow and develop into what they want. The story of others is also inspirational to those you are leading and sometimes more inspiring than your own, because often they still have difficulty believing you weren't always as good and as polished as you appear now. For example, when I share with audiences that I am naturally introverted and shy, and that it was very hard for me to talk to people when I first started, often they look at me in disbelief. Over time as they get to know me they begin to understand that it's true, but it is not immediately inspiring because they can't see it. There are two kinds of stories that serve this purpose. The first are stories of people outside of networking who have overcome difficulties and struggles to achieve something significant. These real life examples display the power of human will and determination and help people begin to see their struggles as smaller than they previously believed. When the mountain begins to look smaller, the belief that it can be climbed grows. The other source of stories you should use are those of people who are in the network who are overcoming struggles. Be careful with this one because you have to be wary of the comparison issue (I talk about this later). Pick examples that relate to their struggle and are either hugely successful now or are achieving small success that is relatable to their current level in the business. The hugely successful ones example the big picture of what's possible from humble beginnings and the small successes demonstrate something they can reach for right now. Both of these inspire differently, but the key is that they inspire.

When the mountain begins to look smaller, the belief it can be climbed grows.

Having helped someone be inspired is the start. Having them be empowered such that they move forward boldly is how the inspiration becomes *productivity*. For this to happen, they must begin to develop belief in themselves. Never forget that most people look in the mirror and see what they don't like. In a practical sense this means they see their limitations and weaknesses. They think about what they *wish* they had from a personal perspective.

Few people ever assess their strengths and gifts. They don't know all the great attributes they have that can lead to success. When I conduct strengths and weaknesses exercises with groups, I allow several minutes for them to think about what their strengths are and only a few minutes to assess their weaknesses. Why do I do this? Because people have been studying their own weaknesses and using them as limiting beliefs their entire lives. It only takes them a few minutes to create a list as long as their arm of all the things they feel that are weaknesses.

People have been studying their own weaknesses and using them as limiting beliefs their entire lives.

Uncovering their strengths is like pulling teeth! They sit puzzled for a few minutes. They struggle with what their strengths *are* and whether thinking about what is good about them makes them boastful or self-centered. It's interesting that no one thinks focusing on personal weaknesses is self-centered isn't it? Anyway, after a bit of coaxing they begin to think about all the skills they have, the knowledge they possess, the positive personality traits they have, the things they are good at doing, their various accomplishments large and small, and before you know it they are beginning to smile. They are realizing that they aren't so bad after all! Jim Rohn often said "your gifts will make room for you." What he was saying is a paraphrase of a proverb which means your gifts, or in this case your strengths, are all you need to achieve your dreams. This is what you are supposed to use. It is how you were made. You don't fight how you were made. You embrace it and develop it and flourish with it!

By helping the people understand their strengths and how they will apply in building their business you have given them the ultimate in empowerment. You have helped them see that *they are good enough to succeed*. You have helped them understand that they have what it takes. It won't happen overnight though. Just helping them see this and reinforcing how they will use this in the day to day effort of growing a business doesn't mean they will be bold and powerful now. It will help them to have enough self-belief to take a step. You will have to constantly remind them that they have what it takes. Empowerment of an individual is also a process. The more often you help them discover what they are capable of, the stronger they will become, the more steps they will take, and eventually they will be strong enough and empowered enough to deal with the ups and downs and the negativity the world will throw at them.

Consider some of the people you are working with in your organization. What are their strengths? What stories would connect with them?

Coaching in Leadership

Coaching is a big part of successful leading in networking. You will be working with people who all are unique. You can't just say the same things to everyone and you cannot just tell people what to do. Instead you have to use a process of mutual discovery. I have a certification in coaching because I wanted to learn how to do it the best way possible to serve the most people. However, you do not need a certification to effectively coach and mentor in the networking world. You just need a simple framework for the dialogue that helps someone understand how to move forward or how to overcome situations that challenge them. Coaching as a leader is different from being a professional coach. In a classic coaching relationship, you have no investment in the outcome or future results of the person you are coaching and you don't offer advice. This excerpt from *The Business and Practice of Coaching* explains this clearly: "The coaching relationship is one of partnership and collaboration. Although the coach may be an expert in certain skills or areas, as a coach she positions herself as an equal with her clients. She asks perceptive questions rather than gives advice. Her clients define their own goals, choices, and decisions with her input."* When you are coaching someone in your network this is not completely true. You are an expert and your advice matters and is often needed. Even though your intention is to help this person succeed, there is still the fact that you also benefit from that success. As you can see, leadership coaching is a different type of coaching. Here is a simple framework for helping to develop people through the coaching process that is specifically for coaching from a leadership position. When you train someone to get started, this is an event. Coaching is a process. You deliver information that teaches and enlightens in training. In coaching you work together to help someone own the outcome and develop platforms of understanding that lock in the learning.

Here is a basic outline you can follow:

1. Ask questions to determine exactly what the actual problem or issue is. The first thing they tell you will not likely be the real problem. It will be the

result of the problem. You are not helping them correct the result. You are helping them to correct the true problem which is creating the result.

2. Praise them for their efforts. You wouldn't be in the discussion if they weren't making an effort, so help them to feel good about this. They have taken some action. This is the key to success. They need to understand that they are demonstrating a willingness to do what they need to do. Most people struggle with esteem and confidence so use this as an opportunity to build them up.

3. As they are answering your questions, you will know quickly what the real issues are. Do not tell them immediately; instead ask them further questions to help them reveal the real issue to themselves. Often they will come to the answer you would have given them. When this occurs, they have ownership in the process and their confidence increases. If they cannot get to the answer, at that point you share your perspective based on your experience.

4. Once you have broken down all the issues, and made adjustments, encourage them to continue doing what they are doing, only now they will be working in a more effective way.

5. Remind them that you are available for them and that they can reach out to you whenever they have a question. You only ask that they think through what they should do before bringing the issue to you. This demonstrates ongoing support and gives them more confidence to take more steps.

6. Set a time in the next week or ten days to discuss and review and debrief their work. This serves as an accountability step that increases the likelihood that they will continue to take action.

This is a very simple way to become effective in coaching people. Recognize that the key component in coaching is *asking questions*, not telling them what to do. You are creating self-sufficient network marketing business builders that can go on to be leaders if they desire. Not only are you helping them, but you are showing them how to help others by using this process. Effective coaching will require you to use empathy, encouragement, and praise throughout. At any time during the discussion you can also share your experiences in similar situations, and also your failures along the way. This further assures them because they didn't consider that you also had struggles in your business as you grew. They will feel more connected to you and understand more clearly that they are on the right track.

Who in the organization needs a coaching discussion now?

"It's Not Working"

You will hear 'it's not working' (or something like this) frequently in network marketing, especially with newer people. Another phrase that is similar is "no one is interested." As a leader who is building an organization, you know these are not the real issue. You know the business works. You know people are interested. However, you cannot just say this to the person who is expressing this to you or you will miss the opportunity to help them. You would be discounting their feelings and/or assuming you know the problem. Instead you have to dig in with this person and help them see what the real issue is. This is usually not often a true coaching situation as much as it's a short dialogue to create understanding. I'll use a real example to give you a framework for how to work through this with someone to help them see the real picture.

Mary (not her real name) comes to me and says the business is not working. I say, "What do you mean the business isn't working?" She says that she has contacted a lot of people and no one is interested. I say, "Let's talk about it for a few minutes" and then I ask "How many people have you contacted?" She says 32. Okay, so now I say, "So you have talked to 32 people?" And she says, "Well, I haven't talked to them all yet." Now I have something to work with because I know there is a difference between what she initially said and what the reality of the situation is. So I ask her to break down for me how she contacted the people and how many she has had an initial conversation (approach) with. She tells me that she has emailed 14, left voice messages with 11, and talked to 7.

What's important to understand at this moment, is that Mary *thinks* she has approached 32 people, when in fact, at the moment, she has only approached 7. I don't say this yet, I take my questions a little further first to help her get a complete picture. So now I ask her about the 7. My first question is 'Mary, how many of the 7 have told you no?' She says that one person has told her no. Then I ask her to tell me about what is happening with the other six people. She tells me that she sponsored one, and that the other five are still reviewing information. So now I have the truth about her actual numbers and I can discuss with her what is really going on. I can share with her that out of her first 32 people ONLY one has told her no! I can review with her the human nature numbers that of any population of ten people who have a need, two will be ready to act on that need. I can show her that in fact, she has only shared with 7 people and sponsored one, so she is right in line with those numbers. The business is working exactly as it typically does. It is her *perception* of what is happening that is the real issue.

It is her perception of what is happening that is the real issue.

The next thing I will do is break down for her the emails and the voicemails, to make sure she is doing those the most productive way possible. I will ask her to tell me, or show me an email, so I can coach her on how to best contact by email to ensure a response. Then I will ask her to share what kind of message she left on the voicemails, so I can coach her on how to leave the right kind of voicemail to ensure a high percentage of return calls.

It is normal for people to not follow exactly what you teach in the process. In this case I will praise Mary for taking the action of reaching out to the first 32 people on her list. I will help her see that she is on track with her numbers and at the same time I am able to have her show me where her misconceptions and errors are. She is fully participating in this conversation and has ownership in the outcome and is on more solid ground to move forward productively as a result. In this case Mary was excited to move forward and has since developed into a successful leader.

How often have you heard this and how have you handled the situation?

Comparative Caution

Comparison is a slippery slope for both you and the people you lead, and you should avoid it except when it provides inspiration. Leaders are doers. They are goal setters and goal achievers. It is natural to look around and see what other achievers are doing and it can be valuable in the proper context. There will always be people building their business faster than you. There will almost always be people who are at higher ranks than you or who are earning more money than you (except for the rare occurrence when you are the single top producer in your company). There will also be many people who are not yet achieving at your level.

Earlier I mentioned people are running their own race, and of course you are running *your* own race. Therefore you are working in your own way and paying attention to the things that are important to you in the process of building your business. They are two sets of issues (besides attitude) that impact someone's big picture business production: Priorities and skills. As a leader you have already developed the skills to build your business to whatever level you would like (when I say skills I am not discounting personality qualities, I am assuming these are wrapped into the skill development for the sake of simplicity in this discussion). This means that the greater influence on how big of a business you build, and at what speed, will be driven by your priorities. Given that two people have identical skill sets, the one who works more will build bigger and faster. What you don't know when you look at other high achievers is what their priorities are. You don't know what they value and you are not inside their life to see all aspects. This is why comparing yourself to others who are more successful in the business isn't sensible. You simply do not know their entire story. They are not in your life and you are not in theirs. As long as you are accomplishing what is important to you in the big picture, you are on the right track for you. Remember, leadership is not predicated on your position, but more on who you are in combination with your achievement.

Comparing yourself to others who are more successful in the business isn't sensible. You simply do not know the entire story.

The place to look to others who are high achievers is in how they work and what characteristics they display that you feel are worthy of emulation. This is how you can make comparison a beneficial thing. You can help yourself to be better, but better in who you are and how you work, not in trying to be better than them. You only want to focus on being a better YOU today than you were yesterday. This is the right way to use comparison as a tool. Comparing purely on a production basis will either deflate you (because others are achieving more) or it will create pride (because you are doing better than others) which tends to lead to a "know it all" type of self-importance. Neither of these is helpful to building your future.

You only want to focus on being a better YOU today than you were yesterday.

When you are leading and mentoring others be careful in how you use comparison. To talk about how someone else is achieving more than the person you are mentoring will only lead them to further doubt themselves and question if they have what it takes. Remember, the people you are working with do not naturally see all the good qualities they have. They see what they think are their limitations and weaknesses. Comparing them to others will usually lead them to think about how they are not like the other person and therefore will never be able to have the same success. To use comparison effectively with the people you are leading, point out to them the qualities they have that others are utilizing to be successful. This helps them see that they CAN be successful being who they are.

Who can you use as a specific positive comparisons for the people you are closely working with?

Dealing with Conflict

Perhaps you had the impression there is no conflict in a network marketing business. Maybe you thought because this is such a cool business where people are inspired, positive, respectful, encouraging and helpful that everyone is just happy all the time and never is heard a discouraging word. Sorry to burst your bubble! Conflict is a natural part of life. Any time you have people working together for any given amount of time, regardless of how nice and respectful they are as people, you will eventually have conflict of some sort. Since there is going to be conflict it's important to have some insight on how to handle it for the best possible outcome. Conflict can be a very good thing if handled properly or it can be very damaging. As a leader you will be involved in conflict with others and you will also be involved in conflicts between people in your organization.

To start with, there are a few things to consider in your approach to the situation. First, learn to welcome conflict. Not only is it a natural thing but it shows that people care. If they didn't care, there could be no conflict. You want caring people. You want passionate people. You cannot have this without also having conflict. It is also a learning opportunity for you and those in the conflict. Second, give people the *benefit of the doubt*. Believe that their intentions are pure. This will allow you to have a more positive approach. The positive approach will help ensure that you do not become emotionally charged. You must keep emotions out of it so that the focus is on the i*ssue and not on the person.*

Learn to welcome conflict. Not only is it a natural thing, but it shows that people care.

To be effective in navigating conflict, it's necessary to know how it evolves. All conflict starts with a difference of opinion. Since we all have differing opinions with others frequently, this guarantees the possibility of conflict. The problem arises when the opinion is not respected. A behavioral fundamental I consistently preach in networking is to be respectful. You don't have to agree with someone, but you should respect their right to their opinion. In the process if you aren't respectful of the people who are not ready to join your network or use your product, you will create ill will and a lasting negative opinion about you and your company. In this case, we are talking about respect among the people who are working in the organization. Since they are from all types of backgrounds and have their own set of values as well as their own reasons for building a business, there will be frequent differences of opinion on all kinds of aspects of the business. When there is respect, there won't be conflict. However, the minute someone feels disrespected, the situation will begin to escalate. The issue will cease to become the issue, and the lack of agreement will now become the issue. It becomes personal and this is where it can fester and become a very negative influence in the organization as a whole. As a leader, you need to be aware of where and when this is taking place and monitor the situation. When it becomes a full blown argument, this can have lasting negative consequences. Unlike a typical work place setting where the issue is right in front of everyone and it has to be resolved, a network is made up of self-directed entrepreneurs who don't have to see this person all the time and don't have to work it out if they don't want to.

Unfortunately, depending on the size of the issue, this can breed the type of negative talk or actions that can affect many people in the group. People will try to sway others to their side of the issue, which generally means they are speaking poorly about the side they disagree with. This can affect the environment at events and fracture working relationships. So what do you do?

In networking you have three primary options. The first is to assess whether or not the parties are truly trying to work it out. If this is the case, then you do nothing but monitor the situation. If it has escalated to the point where bad-mouthing is occurring in the network, you will need to have a discussion with each party to communicate how damaging this is to the organization as a whole and to their own personal businesses. People have enough conflict in their everyday lives, if the network community becomes negative, they will choose to leave and go somewhere else, or they will withdraw and not be a contributing part of the community. Either outcome is a negative outcome. The parties involved in the dispute, are not thinking about this because it is personal to them, so they do not consider the effect on the overall organization.

If the two sides are trying to work it out and not having any success, then the next step is to have a coaching discussion with each party to help them through the process. Follow the coaching guidelines discussed earlier. The basic format will work well for dealing with this issue, but you need to spend a little time helping them understand the importance of a resolution and involve them in the process of figuring out the best answer.

If they still cannot come to an agreement or cannot agree to disagree in a nice way, then your other option is to offer to mediate a discussion between the two sides with the goal of a final resolution. They don't realize how much this negative energy is hurting their ability to work effectively in building their own business. In a mediation type discussion, your role is not to solve the problem for them, and it is not to take sides, as this will alienate the other side and diminish your ability to lead them in the future. Your purpose is to help them resolve the issue.

Resolving conflict in a network is very delicate because there are no real formal consequences you can reinforce. You must already have a strong leadership role with each party in order for your voice to matter, since neither side has to work it out. The only area where there are potentially formal consequences is when the conflict arises over unethical behavior or blatant violations of company policy, in which case this is a matter for the company to hear and not you.

When the conflict involves you directly, the best thing you can do is approach it quickly and with humility. Often a disagreement with the downline will be initiated through a lack of understanding by the lesser experienced person. It will be tempting for you to just squash this with your experience and knowledge. This might work with some people, but it is much better to let them know you are sorry that there is an issue and you'd like to talk about it to see how you can address it and then hear them out, respectfully. A good question to ask is "what is the problem as you see it?" This is a simple open question that gives them the opportunity to express. Sit quietly and let them share completely. Then use clarifying questions and empathy to smooth the road.

Is there conflict currently in your organization which you need to proactively address?

Protecting the Asset

Perhaps you have never considered this or maybe you already know this, but I would be remiss not to talk about it, so here goes. Building a successful network marketing organization means you have created a revenue stream (business volume) and an income stream (monthly profit after your expenses). You have created something of value. The larger it becomes the more valuable it is. One of the definitions of the term asset is *an item of ownership convertible into cash*. Owning a home is an asset. If you sold your home you would convert it into cash. It is a resource. So is your business. The larger your business gets the greater *asset value* it has.

In the case of a network, the asset is uniquely valuable in that it has an element of passive or residual income. The greater the size of the network, the more of the income that comes to you passively. In other words, you develop an income stream that comes to you on a monthly basis regardless of your own efforts. Passive income vehicles usually come from substantial financial investments. For example, if you invested in an apartment complex that has a positive cash flow every month after expenses, this income has a passive nature to it. You took the risk up front to buy the building and establish the operating budget to maintain it, and you receive the rents each month from the tenants. You don't recreate this every month as it is based on leases that have an established length. You don't walk away from it so it's not permanent, but you have the asset that is producing cash flow each month and at the same time you are reducing the debt (mortgage) and the asset is appreciating (gaining market value).

Most passive income assets outside of networking require significant investment capital and or financial risk, or are created by people who have leveraged their talents to create something that produces royalty style passive income like music and books. There are others of course, but these are the best known. In building your networking passive income you are creating a passive income using purely your time and efforts. Essentially, it is all "sweat equity!" Think about this, what would it take in financial resources to have a passive style income of $500 per month? Depending on the vehicle you were using, it would take several hundred thousand dollars of investment capital. Now imagine what it would take to build the kind of passive income that network marketing leaders enjoy? $5,000, $10,000, $20,000 per month and a lot more would require into the millions in financial assets to produce this.

You have, or are creating, a substantial asset. You might not ever want to sell it but you could. In this light, it is important that you understand completely that you have something valuable and that you need to protect it much like you would any other asset. If you have a home, you have homeowners insurance to protect the asset's value should something happen–like a fire or a flood. If you have a store front, you have insurance for that as well. There is no network marketing insurance that I know of, but there are definitely things you can do to protect your asset.

As a leader, this starts with protecting yourself from anything that can diminish your leadership position within the organization, since the relationships and loyalty in the organization are like the mortar between the bricks. The internet has made it pretty hard to hide your success. Once you have developed your organization to a size that displays your abilities and your leadership prowess, you will immediately become a target for other companies that want to shortcut their path to success by bringing in people like you. You will be contacted by other networks who will attempt to entice you to change to their company. They know they can grow quickly by bringing in established leaders who already have networks in place. This strategy is an effort to bypass the phase in all long term companies where pioneering to prove the validity of your product, concept, and management team takes place. A high percentage of all companies don't last very long, and this strategy allows the owners and the early movers to make money before the burden of proof. When they fail (80% of all businesses fail in the first 5 years, and 80% of those that make it 5 years fail by the 10th year) the majority of the leaders who moved their network are now without an income. But worse, *they have lost the credibility they took years to establish.* The bankrupting of their credibility is a major loss. These outfits will promise you the moon and stars. They may even offer to pay you to switch. They will also point out how their company will take all of your people anyway, so you need to act quickly or you will lose what you have. They are good at stirring your emotions and you might be tempted, so I am sharing this as a strong warning that this could destroy the asset you have toiled long and hard to build.

Not only should you avoid these false prophets but you should be careful how you associate with any of the people who are involved. Remember, you are under a microscope and *any questioning of your allegiance* will negatively affect your ability to lead.

There will be other companies that tell you that their business will complement yours and that you can build it within your current network. Doing this will have the same result. You will have caused the organization to question your loyalty and also split your own focus. The Russian Proverb says, "If you chase two rabbits, you will not catch either one." Very few people are successful serving two masters.

In addition to protecting yourself, you must be protective of your network itself. Here are a few basic things to do:

Educate: True success in anything of value in life takes time and development. There are no shortcuts on the road to long term success. The process of growing and developing a long term stable business requires continued commitment, relationship building, and continuous learning. You may already understand this, but many of the people you are working with to grow their business do not. You will need to educate them and develop relationships of mutual trust. The more you invest your energy in helping your people develop and the more you educate them on the true process of success, the less vulnerable they will be to outside influences.

Shield: If you have any question about the motivation of someone else who wants to be involved in your group you must keep them out. Do not invite outside trainers into your group unless you are certain of their motivations. This is also true of working with sidelines. You must be certain of the person you are working with and that they are fully committed to your company before you should expose your organization to them.

Protect the Goose: Your Company is a community of people who aspire to live a better life and help others do the same. You are now a recognized leader in this community. Leadership in a community carries a broader range of responsibilities that relate to the good of the entire community. This means understanding and advocating the policies that are in place to protect the long term interests of the community. Things like product claims, income claims, and employment claims, advertising, dealing with the media, random mailings, etc. are all issues that represent potential pitfalls for the community. Your role in leadership includes knowing the policies and being an example for how to preserve the business and product opportunity for others into the future. This can be a gray area sometimes, especially working internationally with regulations that differ from country to country. Review the terms and conditions to be certain you understand them fully. Without the Goose (Company) there can be no golden eggs (Passive style income stream).

What would it take in investment capital (outside of networking) to create the passive style income you are working to create?

Team Spirit

Team building is an important leadership skill, but in the context of a network marketing organization it is a bit of a misnomer. One of the things that is essential in defining a team is having a common purpose. In a network you have a common purpose in that everyone is striving to build their own business, but they are not working with a true common purpose in that they all are working towards different size goals. The other aspects of a high performing team are that people of complementary skills with mutual accountability are working together to achieve this common purpose. That is not often the case in a network where you have people who may have the same skill set, or it may be different, but they aren't often working together and they are not accountable to each other. Working together should be a case of the upline and downline relationship, especially when the upline truly embodies the spirit of the business, which is helping another achieve their goals as a component of achieving their own. In general, though, team building in the truest sense is not highly applicable. But, there are situational opportunities to utilize teams and there should be an effort to create team spirit.

The role of the leader is to foster team spirit where the people in the network are encouraging and supporting each other regardless of who is benefiting from the productivity. This can be done through the use of events (both business and social) and social networking sites. It is also a good idea to create an identity for the organization so each person can have a sense of belonging to a team. The organization is never *bigger* than the company, and there is a natural sense of comradery among people in the field because they are all working with the same company. This is a little too big though for most people to feel truly connected to on a day to day basis. Much of the work is being done by individuals working by themselves from their homes. The more you can help them feel they are part of something bigger than themselves and that they are together with others (even when working alone), the easier it will be for them to stay engaged.

The more you can help them feel they are part of something bigger than themselves and that they are together with others (even when working alone), the easier it will be for them to stay engaged.

To use a team concept for events, create a working group that has roles for planning and executing an event. In this case there is a specific common purpose where you can utilize people's gifts and abilities in a complementary way and there is a natural accountability for the outcome. As the organization grows you will also want to create leadership teams that communicate and work together for the benefit of the entire organization. Leadership teams are made up of people who are working for a higher level of accomplishment and are closer to the idea of a mutual purpose since the success of the entire organization impacts the environment in which all the leadership's groups are working.

Another thing that is helpful and fosters team spirit is to create an environment where people come together specifically to work the process together. Team calling is an excellent tool where several people get together (day or evening) in a home or some other location and all make their contacts. This is a very encouraging and supportive environment, tends to be highly productive, and fosters a feeling of togetherness. Another proven idea is to use the "workout buddy" concept. This comes out of the fitness industry. If someone has a workout partner they are more likely to go to the gym whether they feel like it or not, and they tend to work harder because their partner is encouraging them and doing it too. This is a great way to work the process because it creates this same type of energy and commitment in building the business.

Wherever possible involve people to help them feel like part of a team. This is a powerful way to help people feel less *alone* since the majority of the time they are working by themselves from their homes and it helps them have the courage to move forward.

What will you do to foster more of a team environment in your organization?

The Value of Vision

If you have two good eyes, you can see-you have vision. Or in this case, sight. But what if you can't see something with your eyes? Does that mean it isn't real? Not from a leadership standpoint. Leaders can see what isn't visible to others yet. They have the true vision to see what has not become a reality yet.

If you look around you at this very moment, everything you can see and touch at one point did not exist. But all of it was seen. It was seen in the vision of the person who created it. For people without *this vision*, seeing is believing. For people with true vision, *believing is seeing*. The biblical proverb says "Where there is no vision, the people perish." (Prov. 29:18) Without vision, life is no more than the constant struggle to survive day to day. With vision, life is boundless. It is full of countless opportunities and abundance and creative energy.

Leaders must show the way. They must inject belief about what is possible that is far beyond what their followers can see. This is not easy to do and it requires certainty on the part of the leader. A leader must create and constantly cast a vision that is much bigger than individual goals. It must be something of significant meaning that creates such a magnetic force that it pulls others into it and opens up new possibilities as to what life can be.

Leaders must show the way. They must inject belief about what is possible that is far beyond what their followers can see.

In his book *Entreleadership*, Dave Ramsey says "The entreleader is constantly stating and restating the organizations dreams and how their team is going to get there. As a leader, if you are not sick and tired of saying the same thing over and over, you have likely not communicated with your team."* This is a valuable lesson for a leader. You are an entreleader (an entrepreneur and a leader) and therefore have vision. But the people you are leading do not have vision. They did not grow up in environments where dreaming and doing big things was part of their life. They don't work in environments everyday where there is much vision. Their idea of vision is working 40 years and receiving a pension so that they can have the time to do a few things they cannot do now. That is not vision. That is a minimalistic view of life. Life is abundant. They can do and be so much more than they know. You have to help them see this.

You have to be the visionary leader that focuses their attention on all that life can be for them, which they cannot yet see. Much of what I have shared up to this point has positioned you to be able to credibly cast vision. But now, you have to go to the next step. Decide what the vision is that you have for your organization. Decide what the impact is that you are going to make in the world. This is a rallying point. This energizes people and helps them to feel part of something far bigger than themselves. It brings a higher level of meaning to their day to day work in the process. Once the vision is clear for you, you must talk about it constantly. Remember, the people in your organization do not have vision as a general rule. Hearing the vision a few times will have no impact. Hearing it over and over, and seeing your commitment to making it happen, will make it gradually begin to sink in. The more they get the vision in the fabric of their being, the easier the day to day work will be for them. A big vision, that becomes part of the foundation of belief, gives strength and courage and makes the challenges of each day seem tiny in comparison to the possibilities that are opening up.

What is your vision for the impact your organization can make in the world around you?

No Control

Mature leaders understand that they have little control over the actions of the organization. They know that one of the key attractions of building a network marketing organization is the freedom that a successful business affords. The lifestyle potential is a normal thing to promote. The ability to work when you want, with whom you want, from where you want, and as much as you want, are natural aspects that everyone loves about the business. What is less often promoted but equally important is the *way you want*.

I used the word *mature*, because mature leaders recognize that each person is unique and therefore has their own set of talents and abilities to bring to their work. Immature leaders haven't recognized this yet and are consistently trying to put their people into a specific box under the guise of duplication. Because THEY built their business a certain way they try to fit everyone into this style because that is what they believe is duplicable. I call this the duplication myth. People are rarely duplicable. *The process* is what needs to be duplicated because this is the basic fundamental.

Many years ago, I had a group that was growing quickly. They had a technique for building the business that was working very well and they were excited about it. What they were doing was legal and inventive. Unfortunately, I was too immature at the time and I did not handle this the right way. I should have encouraged them and applauded them. Instead, I tried to control them. I tried to tell them how it wasn't exactly what I was teaching and they should change it. *They left the business and I learned the lesson.* This is how life often works. You learn the lesson from the mistake.

How someone works in the process should be open to what is best for the person working it. If leaders try to control exactly how someone works they will end up minimizing their reach because they will push away all the people who don't fit in their same personality and skills box. You want to create an environment that is attractive to all types of people, that is the beauty of the industry. A business that is free of all prejudice. A business where anyone, regardless of background or personal characteristics has a chance to create something special that meets their needs and desires.

How someone works in the process should be open to what is best for the person working it.

There are enough rules in life as it is. As the organization grows, in an effort to manage it, you will be tempted to build in more and more structure and rules. Structure is important because working from home is generally absent of structure and people grow up in a structured world. So having some structure of events and mechanisms for creating and supporting a community is important. However, the more rules you make to control how people work, the more you will create a time bomb in your business. Ultimately, as I spoke earlier about letting people fly, you will have significant pieces of the organization react negatively to efforts to control them. You will be perceived as trying to tell them what to do. They worked hard to be in a position where *no one* tells them what to do. Of course there are company policies by which they must abide, and there are socially acceptable aspects to interacting with the network but beyond this, you have no true control over them and the more you try to control what they can and cannot do, the more they will disown you as their leader and it will fracture the network.

Think of it this way…your best people, your biggest builders, your rising stars, and your future leaders, will all reject any form of control you attempt to place on them. Just like YOU would. So focus on what is important to control, your actions, your efforts, and your availability to support.

Is control an area that you struggle with?

Leading in a Growth Phase

There are times when the organization has rapid growth, or what some would call momentum. This is the easiest time in which to lead. Anyone can get in front of a parade and appear to be leading it! I have been fortunate to have participated in several rapid growth phases in my career. They are incredibly fun times, and make you feel like you can do no wrong. There is a sports axiom that *you are never as good as you look when you are winning or as bad as you look when you are losing.* This applies to business too. During rapid growth, the first rule of thumb to remember is *that you are never as good as you appear when business is booming*!

Every leader eventually has some level of a rapid growth phase at least once in their career.

Rapid growth occurs because a lot of people are excited and taking action at a high level at the same time. It will build on itself for a while because the increase in overall action will lead to an increase in overall results (volume) which increases pay checks, which further instigates more excitement and more action. Every leader eventually has some level of a rapid growth phase at least once in their career. Often the leader has tirelessly laid the groundwork and is responsible for getting the ball rolling. But the reality is that *momentum cannot come from one person acting alone.* Thus, the leader may have been the catalyst but the organization is making it happen. So should you find yourself in a period of rapid growth, here are four things to make sure you do:

1) **Be "seen" working alongside everyone else:** Get in the trenches and model the same activity the organization is doing. Recognize the season, and be available more than ever to support. If it is perceived that you are *riding* on them and not working too, this will cause them to slow down and think they can ride too. You never want to do anything to slow it down before it does so naturally.

2) **Stay out of the way:** You were leading the parade and then the parade started going faster, getting faster, still bigger, still faster. Do you keep running in front of the parade? No! Now is the time to get out of the way. Let them run. Let there be fun-filled chaos, let others see that its wide open in front of them-THEY can be in front. It took me until about my third rapid growth experience to finally learn this lesson (Yes, I am a slow learner). Now is not the time to direct or instill new programs, or create more structure. LET THEM RUN. As a leader you should be looking ahead, looking across, looking for who needs help, and looking forward to see where they are going. If they are, as a group, beginning to head in the wrong direction, you will then need to step forward to make some adjustments. But let the chaotic pace go for as long as you can and don't do anything to confuse it or disrupt it. Think about what you might do to extend the momentum or how to build on it in the future when the organization begins to fatigue. But in the midst of the run, be less visible in the front.

3) **Stay humble:** I have seen so many leaders in my career who got big-headed in times of growth. They instantly developed the mindset that they were better than others. That THEY were the reason for the growth. They began to "know it all" and behave arrogantly. Momentum doesn't last forever. It's just a season in the business. Hopefully you will experience it multiple times in your career, but it is never a permanent condition. This is when you do your best to deflect recognition and shine it on those in the organization who are making it happen in the field. Nelson Mandela said "You see, when there is danger, a good leader takes the front line. But when there is celebration, a good leader stays in the back room. If you want the cooperation of human beings around you, make them feel important. And you do that by being humble."* When you are recognized, say "thank you, but this is not about me. I'm fortunate to serve amazing people. They are the ones driving this, not me." YOU recognize THEM

when you are getting recognition. You can foster huge loyalty and good will by remaining humble during the good times. And you need to do this, because you know that what goes up at some point will begin to come down. You will need to have a solid relationship and a strong leadership position to help them through the down phase.

4) **Help Solve Problems:** One of the natural outcroppings of rapid growth is an increase in problems. In general, more people equals more problems! So there will naturally be an increase in "people issues" throughout the organization, and in addition there will be corporate and systems issues as well. Rapid growth puts a strain on resources. When growth accelerates, everything is being utilized at a higher rate which creates an accelerated need for more resources. It is a great challenge to have, but it is still a problem to solve. Since accelerated growth is not predictable most of the time, the company will tend to be behind the growth instead of in front of it. Back-orders can begin to happen frequently as the company runs through inventory more quickly, suppliers go through raw materials more quickly, and manufacturers aren't currently producing levels in harmony with demand. Customer service will become overwhelmed as call volumes grow beyond the current staff's ability to efficiently handle it. New customer support staff will need to be added and placed into the work flow much quicker than usual which means training times are reduced which means mistakes will grow at the customer service level. Suddenly, it will seem that there is a dramatic increase in problems. In actuality, the percentage of problems has increased by a small amount but the amount of problems *has* increased substantially. This will slow the momentum if it's not handled properly by the company and the leadership in the field. Keep in mind that *problems are opportunities dressed in work clothes!* They always have been and they always will be. You must champion the company in this period and also be the chief problem fixer. The organization, especially the newer people (and they are the biggest part of your business in rapid

growth), don't understand that this kind of growth creates temporary problems while the resources are brought up to the level necessary to support and sustain the growth. You need to promote and educate on how good it is to have these problems, that the company can be counted on to do the right thing (after all that's how they got into a position to even have rapid growth!), and that the problems are only temporary. People will be patient if they know what to expect. Think about it, people wait an hour and a half to eat in popular restaurants! The next best thing you can do is take the responsibility to solve as many challenges in the field as possible. You want the organization to keep working at the accelerated rate as long as it possibly can. If you intercede and handle as many problems as you can, this will allow the teams to keep growing and it will demonstrate that you are there to serve them and that you are there when it seems they need you most. You will further cement your relationship and leadership position by showing them you can be counted on. This will serve you very well in the future.

What will you say when you are recognized publicly for the achievement of your organization?

Leading Through Plateaus

Plateaus are periods of time in a business, industry, and organization growth cycle when the movement is generally sideways on the growth curve. For example, if you look at an historical perspective of any financial market, you see extended periods where the graph goes up and down over a period of time but stays within a certain range, where it doesn't go up or down much beyond a certain point. It's as if there is a floor and ceiling and the graph bounces between them, with a gradual trend towards growth (for expanding markets). This happens in a network marketing organization as well. The larger the organization gets the more likely it plateaus more often than not, because there will be organizations within the organization that are growing, stagnating, and declining, and they will balance out somewhat. Leaders understand that this will happen. They know that there is no such thing as straight up continuous growth.

After an extended period of rapid growth, the organization will reach a peak and then it will fall back some. The degree of the fallback is dependent on multiple factors, including the type of business model. Models that are driven by large up front purchases will have a much steeper drop than ones driven more by a true consumer purchase level of sponsoring. This is because the consumer volume will represent a larger portion of the overall volume when growth slows.

The self-evidence created by a momentum period makes it easier to sponsor because prospects can see the activity and feel the excitement of the organizations movement.

Sponsoring is the key factor. Sponsoring is the highest energy activity and momentum is fueled by accelerated sponsoring rates. The self-evidence created by a momentum period makes it easier to sponsor because prospects can see the activity and feel the excitement of the organizations movement.

They are attracted to this and at the same time don't want to miss-out on something so many other people are doing. New people have higher sponsoring rates in momentum times than any other time. At some point the sponsoring rate begins to slow (it's actually just becoming more normalized where it might be closer to 2 in 10 sign up as opposed to higher in momentum) and at the same time the organization begins to *fatigue*. It's unnatural for human beings to maintain high energy for extended periods of time without getting tired. Especially high energy and excitement. Adrenaline for too long leads to exhaustion. This is exactly what happens to an organization. It will naturally have fatigue periods after intense periods of effort. There are lots of other factors that can slow momentum as well. A new competitor in the market, the season of the year, an issue in the environment you work in (economic, political, regulatory, etc.), are some potential factors. The point is that eventually momentum slows, there is a fall back, and the plateauing period will begin.

A plateau can also occur in young organizations. They start to grow- sometimes quickly, capitalizing on the *low hanging fruit* in their close circle of influence. They may grow month after month for 3 to 6 months, and then they hit a ceiling and they plateau for a while. Usually this happens because the majority of the initial growth is driven by the high activity of just a few people and then it reaches a point where the organization is big enough where those few cannot have as big an effect because their activity is now a much smaller percentage of the overall volume.

So now you have some understanding of plateauing, and are probably thinking "I get that, because I have spent quite a bit of time there in my business!" You have if you've been in the industry for more than a few years (unless you got started in the midst of a momentum run and it hasn't slowed yet) and have built any level of a business. It's a necessary part of all businesses and life. All things plateau. You plateau in your own development as a person. You grow and then feel stuck for a while. By continuing to work and persist, eventually you will break through the glass ceiling and grow until the next developmental ceiling and the personal development plateaus all over again.

True leaders show up big time during plateau phases. They know this is the best time to invest in the organization they serve. This is when you stand strong in the front and inspire and encourage. I said that anyone can get in front of a parade and look good—but only true leaders will step up when it's difficult.

Only true leaders will step up when it's difficult.

The lesson here is to keep it real with the organization. All businesses that succeed (with the occasional exception) grind out their success day in and day out. Plateau phases are just more representative of true business. Long term plateauing in successful organizations will have an UP trend. There are many highly successful companies in the world who never had a rapid growth phase. People should expect to take three to five years to build the foundation of a successful business. As a leader you have to manage the excitement of the possibility of rapid growth with the reality of building a true business. It is your role to drive the long term message into the organization.

As a leader you have to manage the excitement of the possibility of rapid growth with the reality of building a true business.

During these times you will do a lot of coaching and supporting in a very hands on way. You will need to continuously cast vision about what is in front of the organization. They will be focused on the day to day emotions and activity of growing a business. They will need to be reminded of the big picture. You are the one who can credibly share this. Remember to share your struggles from your past. This will serve as a breath of hope for them. True leaders become much more visible in times of plateau.

Think of it this way. A time of working through a plateau is when you discover who your long term players are. This is an opportunity to build the foundation with the right people and position the organization for the next phase of growth. Those that work through the plateau will be best positioned to benefit the most when the next growth phase comes.

Who are the people in the organization that you can develop to lead the way for the next growth phase?

Heart and the Crystal Ball

It would be wonderful if we had a crystal ball when we sponsor so that we could see who will become the next successful leader in the organization. Since we don't, all we can rely on are some basic characteristics that we deem important in building the business. At this point, it should be clear that anyone who *chooses* to can become a leader. They simply have to develop themselves and their credibility while they do the work, in addition to having the desire to lead.

From my perspective, the first and most important things I look for are kindness, honesty, and respectfulness. These are absolute musts in growing and eventually leading a network. From these three fundamental behaviors, anyone who is diligent can grow a business and a platform for leadership. Are there any other things to look for? Yes, there are. An obvious one is good people skills. These can be developed through the business and personal development, but if they are already in place, it's helpful for someone to be more effective, initially. There are other indicators as well that I will touch on.

Look for people who have had success in something before. It can be anything from athletics, to scholastics, business, or any other type of accomplishment. This reveals a work ethic, self-discipline, and an ability to work through difficulties. Becoming successful in *anything* means you have pushed through the challenges that are part of any journey of achievement.

People who come from military, law-enforcement and firefighting have had to undergo intense and rigorous training that require the development of high levels of discipline and are consistently in situations that demand courage, bravery, and selflessness. These are excellent foundations for developing leadership.

People that work in trades and manual labor know the value of hard work and perseverance and tend to have a natural humility. Also excellent traits for leadership.

People who run small businesses have had to scratch and claw and stretch themselves. They have taken risks and have chosen to believe in themselves. They too have had to persevere, work hard, and show up each day whether they feel like it or not. All of these lend themselves to developing as a leader.

Another good indicator of potential are people who work in arenas that involve serving and teaching. These are people who already invest themselves in others as a way to make their living. They are less self-focused and have an easier time working with people the right way. After all, our entire industry is built on the idea of helping someone else as the way to help yourself.

I could go on and on describing the kinds of people who *could* lead. If I left out your profession it's only because I'm not trying to cover every single one, but rather giving some insight to characteristics that can be revealed by someone's work life experience. All occupations require developing characteristics that can transfer into leadership.

All occupations require developing characteristics that can transfer into leadership.

Another thing to look for is influence. There are people in all organizations and communities who wield influence. They don't have to be in a leadership position. They just have to be someone that others listen to and respect. These people are called influence leaders. They are easy to spot, and they are plentiful.

The thing that you cannot see, that is the most vital thing after kindness, honesty, and respectfulness, is having heart. This is the unknown. People who have the heart to accomplish something will move mountains to do it. Nothing stops them. This means you can never judge a person based on appearance or accomplishment as the true measure because you cannot see the heart. This is why you offer the opportunity to everyone who is nice and honest, regardless of their history, because you just never know what might happen.

There is one thing that can help you get a feel for this, and it's something I look for, and that's a history of adversity. I love to sponsor someone who has been through some really difficult times. People who have experienced significant loss in life, who have had a major failure, or who have worked in professions where they had to take personal risks regularly, have a real understanding of what hard things are in life. Building a network marketing business, and facing criticism or rejection as the obstacle is laughable to this type of person. In his book, *Tough Times Never Last, But Tough People Do*, Robert Schuller stated "The path is called the "Possibility Thinking Path". I've been preaching it for years. It has never let me down. It has never let anybody down. It never quits on us. We may quit the path, but the path keeps on going on to happiness, health, and prosperity."* People who have weathered adversity and continue to pursue opportunities, tend to be people that are willing to walk the possibility path for as long as it takes.

Those who have faced and endured major adversity have a better perspective about life.

I had a discussion not long ago with a dear friend and emerging leader. In his past profession he was a homicide detective. This meant that every day he kissed his wife and children good-bye in the morning, knowing that there was a real possibility he might not come home again. He had to endure countless moments where the negative thing that could happen during work was being killed or injured. Do you think the idea of him hearing the word "no" is scary to him when he looks at it through this context?

Those who have faced and endured major adversity have a better perspective about life. They are happy that the worst thing that could happen in a day of working to build a network is someone may criticize or say no. So look for people who have been through a lot in life. They have a great foundation to build from.

In the long run, you want to be an excellent leader who develops leaders. This is the greatest fruit you can produce in your work. The more leaders you produce the greater your impact will be in the world. Sure, you want to build a successful business, but why not go the extra step and build a legacy? Developing leaders leads to legacy. A legacy happens when the little steps of your humble beginnings leave giant lasting foot prints in the world around you.

Who are the potential leaders in your organization now? Who are the potential leaders you haven't talked to yet?

Final Thoughts

When I first started writing this, I had no idea how much I would share. I have been teaching and doing leadership for a long time. There was so much I wanted to equip you with that I felt a little overwhelmed, but thankfully once I started writing, this book just unfolded itself a little more each day. My goal was to give you the main things that would help you in your pursuit to develop yourself as a network marketing leader. I didn't want to overwhelm you either and write a text book, as I mentioned in the introduction, so I limited the topics to bite sizes that I believed were enough to grasp the concepts and ideas that are most important. Only you can judge if I accomplished my mission.

As I sit here now, putting these final words on paper, I almost can't believe I'm finished but I can't think of anything else that you absolutely need. I believe *the basics are all here.* Everything you've read will be applicable for you, and much of it probably already is. I would encourage you to continue educating yourself on the topic of leadership. Much of what I have shared will help you succeed in leadership in any area of your life. But I am just one voice. Leaders pursue continual learning. Read books from people of all fields on leadership and you will continue to find new wisdom that will help you better serve your organization.

This is an unprecedented time period in our industry. As of now, this industry is approaching $200 Billion in worldwide sales. It has reached the point where it is no longer questioned as a viable way to create a long term income-and it's just getting started. Not only will more and more people be looking to this industry as the answer, but as technology continues to advance, the ability to build a network marketing business in minimal time per week across the world will get easier to do. It will still require purposeful effort, but the ability to do the work will continue to become more streamlined. At the same time, the economic landscape will continue to change dramatically. It will become obvious to everyone that having an income stream from network marketing is one of the smartest things anyone can do to secure their financial future in the emerging home-based world of commerce. If you consider the changes in the world in the past 20 years alone, you can begin to understand the dynamic scope of the changes ahead of us.

In my early days in the field, if I wanted to sponsor someone outside of my area, I would have to contact them by a phone with a cord that was attached to a desk. Typically, I would have to reach them in the evening when they were available to talk on their phone *that was attached to a wall* and talk with them enough to get them interested in learning about the opportunity (which was much more difficult because they didn't know anyone who made money in network marketing and weren't even sure it was real or legal). Then I would have to package up the marketing materials (brochure, video, audio cassette) that I had to purchase in quantity. The next day I would go to the post office and pay to send these materials (which I would likely never get back) and then wait three days for them to receive them. Then I would call and usually hear that they had received them but hadn't had a chance to look at them yet. Each phone call costs money if it was a long distance call. This was just to *begin* the process. Essentially the cost to have information in someone's hands was at least $5 and this was only to find out if they were actually interested! And THAT worked!

Today we can send a text to see when they have a moment to talk. After they reply, we can contact them from wherever we are, have a short conversation, and then press a button to email them the information. Within minutes they have the information and the cost to us is *nothing*. We can do this as many times as we want per day, regardless of what else we have going on in our life and we can do it any time we want to. We can talk face to face with someone on the other side of the world for free. It's easy to work this business now and therefore people will be doing it in greater and greater numbers each year. You are at the beginning of an industry explosion and it costs you virtually nothing to be in this position!

Building and leading a network marketing organization is a lifetime thing. That's one of the great things about the nature of the business. There is no set time or age when you have to retire or when you are no longer capable of helping others as long as you are healthy enough to communicate. You will *do life* together with the people you lead. As in all things, there will be seasons in your work. There will be seasons when you are highly involved and there will be times when you might step back for a while. This will be up to you. You won't have to worry about a pension or retirement income from the government (that is much less than you earned when you were working) because the income stream you create through leading a network can continue on.

Life will happen to you on your journey in network marketing *as it would if you weren't leading in this business*. There will be seasons in your family life that will require more of your attention than at other times. You will be able to devote your time to necessary things when they happen without fear of losing a job or a major decline in income. This business has provided for me at times when I went through deep personal transitions, the death of loved ones, and major health crisis of loved ones. It has been a constant through the challenges, experiences, and transitions of raising children, the transitions of aging parents, sudden life upheavals (like surgery and accidents), and many more things I refer to as *life happening*. Some of these situations required months of attention, some for years, and others just the ability to take the needed time in the moment.

As you grow your organization, you will also be able to experience the fruits of the lifestyle this business provides. If you have younger children you will be able to see all the things they do. You will be able to attend all of their sporting events, their plays and recitals. You will be able to go on all of their field trips. You will be able to turn your attention to them in those priceless seconds when they have something to share that is the most important thing in the world to them at the moment. You will be able to let them see the world if you want to, provide educational opportunities, and expose them to the truth that the world is really a good place. You will be able to travel when you want and pursue whatever interests you. You will live a life with minimal boundaries and live it in an abundant way.

The fruit of leadership is delicious and you can have as much as you would like. You will live the richest kind of life. A life where your rewards come through the enrichment of others. A life overflowing with fulfillment and joyful experiences. Yes, you will work hard for this and I believe I have shared enough that you're clear that it won't always be easy. It's not a fairy tale. It's just a better way to live and work. I am grateful that you have given me this opportunity to share with you. I look forward with great anticipation to your future accomplishment and for the impact you make in this world that *needs people like you.*

My Final question: Are you ready to lead?

Addendum: The Daily Dozen

I mentioned my daily dozen a few times in the book, once as a means of developing myself and the other as a way to pour back into myself. As you look at this list, you will see that it encompasses many aspects of taking care of self which are paramount if we are going to serve and help others. One thing I want to point out here is the impact on our attitude and perspective.

In leadership we are the lighthouse. We are the people others look to for guidance and assurance. Since we are constantly interacting with people from this position, we have to be on most of the time. Every day I wake up, it's a new day. I don't wake up in exactly the same mood every day (even though I have an awesome life). Some days I wake up in high spirits and my mind is moving a million miles a minute with all the positive possibilities of the day. Other days I wake up and I feel cloudy. I am more focused on what I don't like or what I don't see as a good thing in the moment. This is just how I am wired emotionally. Knowing this about myself, and knowing I have a responsibility to be a lighthouse, not just for the organization I serve, but for myself and my family, I have this daily dozen that I do every day that *centers* me. Regardless of how I wake up, when I am finished with my daily dozen, I am in the right frame of mind to serve and lead in a positive and energized way. Here is my daily dozen in no particular order:

1) Affirmations: I have a set of index cards that have positive, encouraging, and empowering affirmations written on them. Some are quotes from various people I admire, and some are simply things that are important to tell myself. I read these every day.

2) Listening: I listen to things that are positive and uplifting. It could be music that's inspiring, or it could be a speaker I am learning from or gives me encouragement.

3) Reading: I once heard it said that "all leaders are readers, but not all readers are leaders." I have no doubt this is true. Books have been my mentors for 26 years and they will continue to be. I read something of value for education and inspiration every day.

4) **Reflection:** I sit quietly and think and journal. This allows me to capture what I am thinking about, be creative, and learn from what is currently going on in my business and my life. It also serves as a resource for the future.

5) **Positive self-talk:** I make a point to speak to myself in a positive way. What we say to ourselves matters. The world will say plenty to us that is negative, and it is up to us to make sure that we hear positive words. I tell myself I can, and I will, and I am.

6) **Spiritual Walk:** I invest in my spiritual life by reading and praying.

7) **Exercise:** It's well known that exercise is good for the body, but not as well known that it is important for the brain. When we exercise we feel better, have high energy, and think more clearly.

8) **Nutrition:** I put great nutrients in my body every day and minimize eating foods that are not healthy. The same is true here as with exercise. Nutrition is key to staying healthy and vital for your brain and mood.

9) **Positive associations:** I purposefully avoid negative people and interact with people who are positive and uplifting because I know how important my attitude is to what I do and the people I touch.

10) **Smile and be nice:** It's difficult to have a poor attitude when you smile. Smiling signals your brain that you feel good. It's also a great thing to do for others. A smile is a powerful tool and I make sure I do it often.

11) **Thankfulness:** I focus on what I am thankful for consistently. It's difficult to be unhappy about what you don't have when you fully understand how truly blessed you are. It has been proven that people who are purposefully thankful for all that they have in life and all they get to experience are much happier than those who are not.

12) **Serve and Give:** Nothing feels better than giving and serving. The smallest things you do for another have a big impact on you.

It's not my place to tell you what you should do. I am just sharing with you my secret to maintaining a high energy and positive outlook in a world that pushes the negative on us every day. Perhaps you only need to do a few of these every day to put yourself in the best possible frame of mind, just make sure you do them! I personally need the whole dozen, but that's okay with me, because I know what it has done for me, so I happily do this everyday. "With the right attitude human beings can move mountains. With the wrong attitude they can be crushed by the smallest grain of sand."-Jim Rohn?

End Notes

Section 2– Ken Blanchard, Leading at a Higher Level, Prentice Hall, 2007 (p. 254)

Section 3– Max De Pree, Leadership is an Art, Michigan State University Press, 1987 (p. 22)

Section 5– Kerry Patterson, Joseph Grenny, David Maxfield, Ron McMillan, Al Switzler, Influencer, McGraw Hill, 2008 (p. 153)

Section 8– Dave Martin, The 12 Traits of the Greats, Harrison House Publishing, 2011 (p. 196)

Section 10– Marcus Buckingham, Go Put Your Strengths to Work, Simon & Schuster, Inc., 2007 (p. 84)

Section 11– M. Scott Peck, M.D., The Road Less Traveled, Touchstone, Simon & Schuster, Inc., 1978 (p. 129)

Section 13– Joyce Meyer, A Leader in the Making, Warner Books, 2001 (p. 157, 159)

Section 17– Stephen M. R. Covey, Rebecca R. Merrill, The Speed of Trust, Simon & Schuster, Inc., 2006 (p.6)

Section 20– Richard Koch, The 80/20 Principle, Doubleday, 1998 (p. 4)

Section 23– Michael E. Gerber, The E Myth, Ballinger Publishing Company, 1986 (p. 11)

Section 25– John C. Maxwell, The 5 Levels of Leadership, Center Street, Hachette Book Group, Inc., 2011 (p. 94)

Section 27– Zig Ziglar's Little Book of Big Quotes

Section 28– John Wooden, Jay Carty, Coach Wooden One-on-One, Regal Books, 2003 (Day 51)

Section 29– Ken Blanchard, The Heart of a Leader, David C. Cook, 2007 (p. 5)

Section 31– Stephen R. Covey, The 7 Habits of Highly Effective People, Fireside, Simon & Schuster, Inc., 1989 (p. 238-239)

Section 33– Lynn Groazki, Wendy Allen, The Business and Practice of Coaching, W.W. Norton & Company, 2005 (p. 26-27)

Section 39– Dave Ramsey, Entreleadership, Howard Brooks, Simon & Schuster, Inc., 2011 (p. 215)

Section 41– John C. Maxwell, The 5 Levels of Leadership, Center Street, Hachette Book Group, Inc., 2011 (p. 91)

Section 43– Robert H. Schuller, Tough Times Never Last, But Tough People Do!, Thomas Nelson, Inc., 1983 (p.30)

Other books by Todd Burrier

THE PROCESS
The easy way to build an income stream for life
The Process was written specifically in the language of a referral marketing business model, but is appropriate for building any direct sales or network marketing business. Anyone who is active in a business involving contacting and communicating with people for the purpose of developing a customer and/or working relationship, and creating the foundation for an organization, can succeed through the practical human principles and fundamentals in this book. Regardless of what type of system your business employs, working the right way with people is a necessity for a long term profitable venture. This is a little book with a big impact!

PROCESS II
Work more effectively and efficiently in referral marketing
"The purpose of this book is to help you maximize the time you have, and to give you the little tips that help you to work efficiently so that you can grow your successful business while still participating in all the other important things in your life. Most of this book is short stand alone ideas and concepts so that you can pick it up and read about things you might need as you work in the process. As it is with all the things I share, nothing in this book is theory. Everything I guide you to do is based on proven experience and will make a difference for you if you implement and adopt the concepts. I hope one day you will wave this book from the top of the mountain of your dreams."-Todd Burrier

LIVE FULL, LIVE WELL

"This is a work of passion for all the people who have sacrificed too much for far too little. It's never too late to change the way you live your life. It's for people who are trying to get it all done but know that every day is just not what it could be. This book is a real, honest, approach to life that can help anyone of any age to have more joy, fulfilment, and productivity in their life through the achievement of balance.

You are going to learn specifically how to develop a balanced lifestyle with this book. You will not read about work-life balance here, because I believe that work-life balance is a misnomer. To even acknowledge the idea of work-life balance is to say that work is equivalent to life. It is not. Life is bigger by miles. There are many aspects of your life that make up what you have to balance. Work happens to be one of them. Work is very important, but so are many other things. You will learn how to balance everything in a way that I have proven to work for over a decade. You will learn how to participate fully in the lives of your children and your spouse, your career, your personal wellbeing, the hobbies and causes you care about, the friendships that matter, and more." –Todd Burrier

THE 6 DECISIONS FOR SUCCESS
MP3

The Six Decisions for Success is an inspirational how-to for anyone pursuing any endeavor. Successfully accomplishing something is truly a choice. There are many aspects to ultimate achievement, from goal-setting and planning, to execution and follow-through. Whatever you endeavor to do and whatever stage of pursuit you are in, you will face difficulty, and usually the degree of difficulty will increase with the size of the goal. Triumphing is about the choices you make along the way. These choices are the 6 decisions. Anyone can succeed. It is simply a matter of following these fundamental truths and deciding to succeed every step of the way!

FOLLOW TODD AT HIS BLOGS:
Toddburrier.com

Here Todd talks about professional success which is about doing work that you love, to achieve your financial goals, without compromising your health, relationships, and values along the way.

THEPROCESSWINS.COM

This is Todd's network marketing blog where he provides ongoing tips, education and podcasts.

Made in the USA
Middletown, DE
27 April 2016